1

The Unconventional Thinking of Dominant Companies

The New Formula for Market Domination

By Jim Bramlett

Dedication

Without my lifelong partner and bride, this book would not be possible. I could write an entire another book on what I put her through via various phases of my career. She always supported me even when I had crazy and bone-headed ideas. She made our family work and though it's not a romantic novel, I am dedicating this book to you Pam. I love you and your patient loving way allowed me to go through experiences that culminated in this book.

I also want to thank my dear friend, author and entrepreneur Robert Ladd for your guidance, editing skills and overall support. You are an inspiration to me and I could not have completed this project without your unwavering support even though you were up to your eyeballs growing your own business. Thank you, my friend.

Acknowledgements

I have always liked surprising my wife. I've surprised her with trips, parties and special gifts. Some of the surprises were quite elaborate and took immense planning. I would include the writing of this book in this category. When I started writing this book I decided that I wasn't going to tell anyone. I largely did that because I have never written a book before and didn't know if I would or could do it. I knew it would take a lot of time and effort and so better to be safe than sorry and keep it to myself.

Once I got organized and decided on the content, it became fun and a mission. However, I never let the secret out except to my friend Robert Ladd who helped guide me on overall process. I decided that I would surprise my wife with the proof copy on a special trip we took to Mexico for a milestone birthday. That's right, I didn't mention the age of this milestone. I'm smarter than you think. Anyway, this trip was special as we decided to take our entire family. We took our three kids, their spouses and our wonderful 6 grandchildren. What better place than to let her know that I had written a book. A real surprise as I don't consider myself a writer, nor even an ardent reader.

I got through the deadlines and ordered the proof and even paid expedited shipping so that the book would arrive before we departed on the trip. In fact, when the book arrived, I quickly opened it, inspected it and placed it safely into my backpack. Whenever I travel, I always take my backpack and this way I would ensure the gift was not forgotten.

However, as fate would have it, when we loaded the car for the airport I forgot to load my backpack. I was so excited about the trip itself and getting our huge suitcases in the car and making the 40-mile trip to the airport in time, I simply forgot it. I didn't realize I hadn't included my backpack until we arrived at the airport remote parking lot and unloaded the suitcases. Immediate panic set in and a few choice curse words shouted without revealing the reason for my attack to my bride. I simply told her I forgot my backpack and had to have it. I finally told her that I had a very important gift for her in the backpack.

I quickly looked at my watch and it was 6:35 AM and we had a 7:50 departure. What to do? So, I did what any guy would do. I called my buddy Bart Bergman. You see, Bart had previously bailed me out years ago when I took my 16-year-old daughter on a vacation and she forgot her photo ID. He rescued us by going by our house and finding her driver's license and speeding to the airport and handing it off just in time. Could Bart do it again? He lives 20 minutes from our house and then a 40-mile drive to the airport and do that in about an hour? I still needed to clear security and get boarded before shutting the door 5 minutes before departure. Let me say this. Bart Bergman should be a Nascar driver. He got it done and for that I am forever grateful. I was able to surprise my wife and entire family and presented the proof in Mexico.

Now of course I had an ulterior motive for taking the proof to Mexico. We were there an entire week and I figured that multiple members of my family would have time to read it and provide me feedback, commentary, check my grammar and help me edit it. So, for that, I want to thank my wife Pam and my daughter Angie for giving me excellent proof-reading services. The others wanted to help but with 6 grand kids under the age of 6 running around, it was a busy and hectic schedule. I love my family and this book is for them.

Table of Contents

Foreword

In my 40 years of working for companies, including my own, I have probably attended 40,000 meetings. Yes, that is an exaggeration but feels it like that. Meetings are crucial to companies coordinating efforts, communicating and being in sync. They also are often a huge waste of time. Now that I work for myself and have no employees, I can be so much more productive.

My experience with meetings is that we typically discuss revenue, budgets, how to cut costs, how to increase sales, how to refine products, add new services, develop new technology, develop new programs, re-organize staff, hire new people, change operations, purchase new equipment and a myriad of other topics.

I don't ever recall a meeting starting like this: "We are here today to figure out how we can make it easier for our customers to do business with us.", or "let's figure out how we can remove the number of steps it takes a customer to buy from us". Never had a meeting where someone wanted to reduce the number of keystrokes to navigate our website. Don't recall any meetings where our sole focus was on developing a mobile app that would take less effort for a customer to enjoy a better experience with our company. Or, how we could layout our store where customers can more easily find what they are looking for and spend less time shopping?

You see, almost all the meetings I've ever been involved with improving internal efficiencies, making more money, spending less, charging more and never has been led by what customers really want. Now, I have worked for a lot of good companies and even a few great ones, but none that are dominant. I define a dominant company as one that has double the market share of their closest competitor and is the most recognizable brand in the industry in which they participate.

You see dominant companies put the customer first in everything they do. They know that if they take care of the customer, the rest will fall in line. It's easy to say, but not easy to do. If you ask any CEO or President of a company, they will tell you they put the customer first, but most of the time, it's just talk. They don't practice what they preach. Good and even great companies take care of customers but don't center every decision they make about how it impacts the customer. Dominant companies do. It's a more natural tendency for good and great companies to focus on the bottom line first. I've heard executives say, "This would be a great company if it weren't for customers." Not exactly putting the customer first with those sentiments.

While they may not admit it, dominant companies use a formula to get to that position. They ensure that they provide the very best customer experience, at the lowest possible cost, while requiring as little time and effort for a customer to engage them. Good and great companies will trade one of those variables off for another. They might give you the very lowest price but trade-off the experience. Or they might give you the lowest possible price but require a lot of time and effort to get that price. Or, they provide an outstanding, incredible experience but their prices reflect it.

Amazon is the very best example of a dominant company using the formula where they don't trade-off anything. They enable a consumer to engage them with little time and effort, have very competitively priced products and the experience has been outstanding, especially compared to competitors. I'm going to cover multiple dominant companies and how they utilize a specific formula to dominate and they never rest. Dominant companies know, especially in today's world, they might be only one innovation away from regressing from dominant to great or good.

A company doesn't have to be large, like Amazon, Uber, Facebook or Google to dominate. A floral shop operating on Main Street, can be the dominant florist in its area simply by putting the formula to work. And, it doesn't take transformative change for many. It can be a series of very small things that can make the difference. It can be simple yet very difficult to go against the grain and do away with the trade-offs and elect to dominate in every element of engaging customers.

It takes an unrelenting focus on the customer and it isn't easy to adhere to the modern formula to achieve dominance. I believe you can boil it down to mathematical formula I dub the Hassle Quotient.

Dominant companies have figured out how to make it easy to be engaged by customers, requiring little time, providing competitive pricing and the best user experience. The dominant companies won't admit or recognize the Hassle

Quotient but when you peel back the "proverbial onion" on how they go about business, they absolutely focus on the customer and enable customers to engage them easier than other companies. I hope you enjoy the book and glean something that you can use in your personal or professional life.

Chapter 1 – The Discipline of Market Leaders

Let me give you a little context so you know where I am coming from. I have been working, at least part-time jobs, pretty much since I was 13 years old. It was the way I was brought up and work ethic was instilled in me at an early age. Back in the day, I was taught that if you work hard, good things would happen. I started my first real job before the personal computer was launched. I love the quote by Lou Holtz that he has written more books then he has read. I'm a bit like that. I love business and love the stories of entrepreneurs of how they started businesses. I enjoy hearing about the failures. A mentor once told me that, to succeed, one must fail. If you don't know failure, you really won't know and appreciate success.

I have seen multiple trends and theories on business. There were two business related books that I read that did strike a chord with me. The first was the EMyth, Why Most Businesses Don't Work and What to Do About It by Michael Gerber. The myth was that owning a business often isn't what one might think. It can often just be buying yourself a job and not giving you the freedom, one might think when owning a business.

The second book and one that really had an impact on me is "The Disciplines of Market Leaders" by Michael Treacy and

Fred Wiersema. The 1997 edition was published before the internet became the mainstay of so many businesses. It was at the forefront of the original dot com era. And, the theories brought forward absolutely, positively makes sense, or made sense at the time when I first read it.

The proposition they support is that no company can succeed by trying to be all things to all people. It, instead, must find the unique value proposition that it alone can deliver to a chosen market. It professed that companies focus on a singular discipline and not try and be all things to all people and the options for the singular discipline were:

- Customer Intimacy
- Product Leadership
- Operational Excellence

Like I said, this book was written before the internet and before companies like Amazon, Google, Facebook, and Uber were founded. I believe the internet has revolutionized how business is now done. It's had a bigger impact than the industrial revolution and even more profound than the computer becoming part of every-day business.

Companies like Amazon are the antithesis of the Discipline of Market Leaders. They do not focus on a singular discipline. They strive to be leaders in every discipline and not just one. They are a dominant company and not just a good or great one. I suggest the internet has changed the rules and now allows many companies to focus on more than just one discipline. It not only allows it, but mandates that companies embrace and adopt all disciplines. A company can focus on one and do fine, but if they want to dominate, they must excel at multiple disciplines.

Customer Intimacy involves the selection of one or a few high-value customer niches, followed by an obsessive effort at getting to know these customers in detail. This requires anticipating the target customer's needs as well as, if not better than, they themselves do, and sometimes sharing risks with them when the development of new products or services is required. The operating principles of this value discipline include:

- Having a full range of services available to serve customers upon demand – this may involve running what the authors call a "hollow company", where a variety of goods or services are available quickly through contract arrangements, rather than the supplier business having everything in stock all the time.
- A corporate philosophy and resulting business practices that encourage deep customer insight and breakthrough thinking about how to materially improve the client's business are essential.

Two companies used as an example back in 1997 were Airborne Express and Nordstrom. Interestingly, Airborne Express doesn't exist any longer. While they might have had some level of customer intimacy, they were acquired by DHL Express in their bid to become the third domestic U.S.

package shipping company. That bid failed and DHL resorted to becoming a leading small package provider of international package shipping. Nordstrom has an outstanding reputation for customer service and customer experience. They have one of, if not the best return policy in retail. They even offer personal shoppers who will get to know you personally and make recommendations to fit your style. Nordstrom shoppers are disciples and advocates and love the experience.

In thinking about customer intimacy in today's world, Netflix, Amazon, and Zappos come to mind. Of course, all of them have a very intensive internet presence and learn about the habits and buying preferences of each customer. Netflix tracks the movies and shows that I watch and then makes suggestions on other shows that I might find interesting. They will email me when such shows are available and freshly released. They are catering to my individual tastes and ask me for feedback on shows and movies so, over time, can improve the recommendations they make for me.

Amazon has done a remarkable job of offering nearly any durable good I could want, they help me make up my mind by recording other buyer experience and have an exceptional return policy. Amazon knows more about their consumer's buying habits and patterns than practically anyone. For consumption products used over and over, one can set up a delivery schedule, and most people know about their passion to deliver within 2 days anywhere and more and more going to same delivery where possible.

Zappos, a company owned by Amazon, is basically the gold standard in customer service. They are known for doing above and beyond for their customers, some of which is outlined in their core values. Their support stores have also reached an almost mythic level. The interesting thing about Zappos is that they're able to deliver on that service across channels. They have live chat, email, phone and social support available 24/7, all backed by their dedicated Customer Loyalty team. And interestingly, but not surprising, Amazon owns Zappos but operates them separately.

Product leadership is the value discipline dedicated to providing the best possible products from the perspective of the features and benefits offered to the customer. Product leadership is based upon the following principles:

- The encouragement of innovation -through small ad hoc working groups, an "experimentation is good" mind-set, and compensation systems that reward success, constant product innovation is encouraged.
- A risk-oriented management style – product leadership companies are necessarily innovators, which requires a recognition that there are risks (as well as rewards) inherent in new ventures.
- A recognition that the company's current success and prospects lie in its talented product design people and those who support them.

- A recognition of the need to educate and lead the market regarding the use and benefits of new products.

Examples of companies that were known as product leaders when the book "Discipline of Market Leaders" was written included Intel, Nike and 3M. With the broad adoption of the personal computer and other various computing products, Intel has been the master at developing and designing computer chips that became more powerful, faster and smaller over time. Nike, mostly known for its wide variety of athletic shoes, expanded into apparel and even into equipment such as golf clubs and golf balls. Interestingly, Nike recently announced they were abandoning the golf equipment space. What will Tiger do? I think he will be just fine. Most people recognize 3M as the innovator of the post-it notes. Even with technology today, those sticky pads still come in useful and 3M is involved in all kinds of products, some consumer-oriented and many targeted to the industrial and manufacturing sector.

Today, I would suggest that companies such as Google, Facebook, and, of course, Apple are product leaders. Google is best known for its remarkable search engine and from there has spun off marketing and advertising services that drive its revenue. However, they created their own cloud-based tools called Google Docs to more easily share with friends and co-workers. They innovated their own email system called Gmail and most recently developed Google

Home, the voice-activated assistant to compete with Amazon's Echo.

Many believe Facebook to be simply a social media platform where friends and family can connect and share updates about themselves. However, as of this writing, the value of Facebook is approximately $435 billion, so it is far more than a free application on the web for anyone to share information. It is a marketing and advertising machine. Via Facebook, a company can learn about target demographics and position ads that target what you are interested in. Much like Google, ever notice that when you search an item or service, you start seeing relevant products and service pop before your eyes in the content you get? Not a coincidence and companies pay dearly to reach consumers with precision-like advertisements. Facebook has branched out to create Messenger and Live and will continue to develop services that can expand their reach.

And then of course there is Apple. When many think of innovation, they think of Steve Jobs and Apple. When Mr. Jobs returned to Apple in 1997, the company was struggling and on the brink of failing. One of the first things Steve did was to assess the projects had in the pipeline. He said; "simplicity and beauty" was the mantra and stopped 90% of those projects. The creation of the iPhone has set in motion a new way to use a computer, a very mobile way. From the iPhone, Apple created the iPod, the iWatch all the while continuing to innovate their Mac series of laptop devices. Apple led the way in how people now listen to music through the innovation of iTunes. Clearly, Apple is a company that today exhibits all the traits of product leadership.

Operational excellence is defined as a discipline whose approach to the market is dedicated to providing the lowest cost goods and services, while at the same time minimizing problems for the customer. This discipline bases its success on several key principles:

- The efficient management of people – employees are trained in the most efficient and lowest cost way of doing things
- The management of efficient transactions – for greater efficiency and speed, processes between suppliers and the organization are often merged (for example, the quality control function, which historically has taken place once by the supplier to ensure a good product leaving their shop, and once at the buyer's end to ensure a good product coming in, is merged into one quality control inspection, undertaken under the auspices of both the supplier and the customer. This reduces cycle time considerably, allowing just-in-time supply and at lower overall cost as well).
- Dedication to measurement systems – to ensure rigorous quality and cost control, businesses dedicated to operational excellence are geared to monitoring and measuring all processes, continually search for ways to reduce cost, and improve service and quality.

- Management of customer expectations – under the principle that "variety kills efficiency", operationally excellent companies provide only one or a limited number of product or service options and manage customer expectations accordingly.

In the Discipline of Market Leader's book, Treacy and Wiersema note that Walmart and McDonalds are two good examples of companies that reflect operationally excellent disciplines. If you are a vendor supplying goods to Walmart, I think you would agree with that statement. If you are a consumer that visits their stores, you might tend to disagree.

Walmart places very stringent qualifications and processes upon their vendors. Not only do they expect the very lowest price point, they demand delivery of product to a very tight delivery window, with very specific labels on the product, stacked a specific way to accommodate their handling procedures and if you fail on any one of those criteria, they fine you. Walmart is all about efficiency in its supply chain. They operate the world's largest private truck fleet and use the fleet to deliver on a timely basis to stores and then pick-up vendor merchandise going back to the distribution center. It is a very efficient operation.

If you haven't had the pleasure of selling to Walmart, let me give tell you a story that I personally experienced. Right out of college I was selling ketchup, cooking oil, tomato sauce, and other key grocery products for a major brand. I lived in Joplin, MO and NW Arkansas was my territory. This was back in early 1977 and I had briefly heard of Walmart but really didn't know much about them as they only had approximately 200 stores. One day I was driving past their headquarters and decided to stop in and see if I could sell them some ketchup. You see, I thought if I could sell them 10 cases per store, that would help me achieve half my quota for the entire year. Was I excited!

I made the appointment and when I arrived was ushered into what seemed like a closet. It was a very small room with no decorations, pictures or anything to resemble an office. It had a table, a chair on the other side of the table and the chair I was sitting in. After a few brief moments, a buyer entered and introduced himself. I made my pitch for Walmart buying the best ketchup in the world and how I was sure every Walmart consumer would want our ketchup on their hot dogs and hamburgers and would increase Walmart sales and profits! Not long after I got started the buyer interrupted me and basically told me what price they would be willing to pay to buy any of my ketchup. Their offer was completely irrational and unrealistic based on other customers I dealt with. Basically, the buyer wanted me to give away the ketchup and the deal never materialized.

A better story. Later in my career I worked for Yellow Freight System and a friend of mine was the Corporate Account Manager whose main responsibility was the Walmart account, one of, if not their biggest shipping customer. As you can imagine, Walmart buys a lot of items to be shipped. They have so much volume that an LTL carrier like Yellow, needs their volume to move trailers on a timely basis to get all freight delivered on-time. Given my personal story, it's probably not a shock to let you know that, at the time, Yellow was losing money hauling Walmart goods. That was okay to a point. So, my friend was instructed to attain a 6% increase in price to lessen the loss. Not to turn it profitable, just lessen the loss. So, my friend strategized for weeks planning on how he was going to achieve this monumental goal of a 6% increase in price, knowing Walmart's reputation for tough negotiations.

Much like me, my friend arrived in Bentonville, AR and like me, escorted into the non-descript closet and waited for the traffic manager to arrive. A few minutes after being seated, the door swung open and a person rolled in a TV with a VHS player attached, plugged it in, turned on the TV and hit the play button on the VHS player and left. Within moments, the video started playing and Sam Walton came on the screen and wanted to thank all vendors for participating in their "Roll Back America" program. Flags were waving, music playing, and this was a 1980's Make America Great Again campaign for Walmart.

When the video quit playing, the monitor was promptly removed, and the door shut. Within five minutes, the door swung open again and, low-and-behold, Sam Walton in person walked in and shook my friend's hand and said he wanted to personally thank Yellow for participating in Walmart's Roll Back America program. My friend was in shock and panic-struck. He was there to negotiate an increase, but Walmart had other plans and was seeking further discounts. Ultimately, due to his skill and determination got a slight increase but nowhere near his goal. Ultimately, Walmart's culture supports their slogan of Every Day Low Prices and in so many ways, operates efficiently. They may have room to grow at the retail level but agree they should remain on the list of operationally efficient companies.

McDonald's is the other company the embodies operational efficiency. While I haven't dealt with McDonald's as a vendor or have stories of others who have, I am certain they are tough negotiators and buy in such volume, their per-unit costs are as low or lower than their competitors. After all, they originated the dollar menu and still must squeeze a profit from those items.

The other remarkable trait about McDonalds is they are a global organization and a Big Mac is going to taste the same in Hong Kong as it is in Chicago, or Berlin or Madrid. In fact, one of my business professors in college stated that McDonalds is known for their "guaranteed standard of mediocrity" when it comes to their food. Many think McDonald's created the first drive-thru restaurant, but they didn't. That distinction reportedly goes to Red's Giant Hamburg (not mis-spelled) in 1947 in Springfield, Missouri. However, they have gone a long way to perfecting it and making it efficient. Along with Walmart, McDonalds still qualifies as an operationally efficient company.

There are a couple other companies that come to mind when I think about operationally efficient companies, one of which

I have worked for, and another their direct competitor, though they operate slightly different business models.

I've spent most of my career in transportation and logistics. After my stint at the major consumer brands company selling ketchup, tomato sauce and cooking oil, I decided I wanted to move back to the town I went to college, Springfield, MO. There I took a job as a management trainee with Roadway Express. Interestingly, Roadway, at the time, would only hire trainees who didn't have any other transportation experience. I thought that was unusual, but come to find out, there is a Roadway "way" and no other, and they didn't have the time nor patience to break bad habits. While I was a green kid, I knew no better. What I did know was that I was getting a 60% raise, (from $10,000 per year to $16,000!). But that wasn't the best part in my mind. I was going to get 26 weeks of vacation per year, or so it seemed. In reality, I got zero weeks of vacation as I was on a shift that worked 7 twelve-hour days and then was off 7 days. The twelve-hour shifts turned into 14-hour shifts and there seemed to be menial tasks I would get called in for during my 7 days off. It was a grueling job, but one that stuck with me and 38 years later, I am still in the business. As a friend once told me, "same ditch, different rut", meaning in the industry, just different company and role.

I probably could write a separate book on the stories and lessons I learned during my relatively short stint at Roadway. After 6 months of 7 days on and 7 days off, I graduated from the trainee program but landed a role that was virtually 6 days on and 1 day off. That wasn't what drove me to change companies, but the culture was. All too often I was stuck in the middle of management and organized labor and it just got to be too stressful. So, I opted for what I thought would be greener pastures. Many of us have been there.

After a particularly grueling night shift, I decided that I would stop by UPS and see if they were hiring. A neighbor of mine worked for them and I liked what he had to say. At the time, everyone who got hired by UPS was inserted as a driver. They wanted everyone to learn the ropes from the ground up. I admired that perspective and though I had no aspirations to be a driver the rest of my career, I didn't have any issues with learning from the bottom up and earning my way into management ranks.

Fortunately, I visited the UPS station when a regional human resources manager was there. I later learned that it was rare to have such a person visiting so I guess fate took over. During my initial interview, the human resources manager made a very strong point that UPS was far different than Roadway. Yeah, I got that. Roadway was palletized freight using big trucks and forklifts and such and UPS was a package carrier. Only later did I learn what he really meant. They made the Roadway "way" look like a hobby when compared to the strict process and procedures that UPS had engineered.

About 3 weeks after my initial interview I received a call on a Sunday night and basically informed me that if I wanted a job at UPS, show up tomorrow morning at 8AM. Gee, I was put in a hard position but was so ready to move on from the harsh Roadway environment that I agreed. Needless to say, the call I placed to Roadway that evening and quitting with no notice was hard. That isn't me, but I felt this was the best option.

Upon reporting to UPS, I was told that I needed to be in St. Louis for 3 days of training and at my own expense, though I got paid minimum wage during the training. That 3 days is where I learned just how "operationally efficient" UPS is. Basically, UPS is an engineering company wearing brown. Every little detail and every action has been engineered. I was taught that as a driver, when you make a delivery you follow these procedures:

1. Upon arriving at your delivery point, honk the horn so they know UPS is here
2. Turn of the engine with your right hand and remove keys and place in pocket
3. With your right foot begin to remove yourself from the seat
4. While exiting the seat, pickup your clip board with your left hand
5. With your right hand pick up the package you are delivering. If multiple, set your clipboard down and then stack packages and place clipboard on top
6. As you exit the package car (yes, they are called package cars), slide the door to the package area close
7. Walk briskly into the business and yell UPS! (I found this humorous because how many other delivery companies have unique vehicles and people wearing

brown uniforms with a UPS logo are running around). I never yelled UPS.

8. Immediately return to your vehicle and look at your packages to see your next stop and repeat steps.

All routes were strictly engineered and on my original route I would make approximately 120 delivery stops per day, deliver maybe 250 packages and then pick up 30-40 stops for outbound packages. Each day, UPS set a "standard", meaning an amount of time that I should accomplish that day's stops, packages and miles driven. If a driver exceeded standard 3 days in a row, you would get the courtesy of a supervisor riding along with you. They told you it was to determine if the standard was too tight, but the real reason was they wanted to check to see if the driver was hustling.

After going through my probationary period and gaining seniority, I was assigned my own route. That was good because I got to know addresses, efficient routes and the best doors to provide deliveries and get to know the customers. However, after a short six months, UPS decided to move 6 routes from Springfield to Joplin. Joplin? Been there and done that. Of course, I was offered the opportunity to move with the work, but they told me not to worry, I wouldn't miss any work. While I thought this would delay my journey to management, I didn't realize at the time that it would bring that aspiration to a full stop.

I began running routes for drivers who went on vacation, typically in the summer. And in the winter would work pre-load, re-load and customer service. All those shifts were four-hour shifts. It seemed like I was regressing toward my goal. However, I got to learn that UPS is equally efficient in all aspects of their operation and not just delivering and picking up packages. Everything is engineered.

So, if there is ever an example of an operationally excellent company, UPS is it. However, that doesn't necessarily translate to lowest cost. UPS is a unionized company and though extremely productive and efficient, they have inherent costs that must be passed along to the customer.

I have never had the pleasure of working for FedEx. Yes, there is a tinge of product leadership and even customer intimacy with them, but deep down they are an operational excellent company. After all, their slogan says it all. "Absolutely, Positively, Overnight." And, they guarantee their service! Do you ever think about the systems, the coordination, the skill it takes to move a package from all corners of the globe overnight, or at the worst in 2 days? Like UPS, everything must be engineered to the 10th degree. Someday I want to tour their sort hub in Memphis in the middle of the night. I've talked to those who have, and it is on my bucket list.

FedEx started by focusing on the expedited/air freight equation while UPS was mostly a ground service. Now, each are involved in all facets of transportation and logistics, though FedEx has multiple companies; one focused on express shipments, one on ground package service and one for LTL freight. UPS has a separate LTL service but integrate their express offering with their ground offering. I don't think anything reflects operational excellence more than the FedEx slogan.

To recap, back in the 90's, Treacy and Wiersma made a great point. A company should really focus on one thing and be the very best at that one thing. Whether they focus on being the most operationally efficient, customer-centric or be a product leader, trying to be more than one will dilute focus and likely result in a level of mediocrity.

Throughout my career I have heard senior leaders of companies state the company had to focus and not chase "shiny objects." The rules about market leaders have changed. A company can focus on a single discipline, be the very best at that discipline, and that doesn't necessarily garner them the position of market leader. The world has changed and there is evidence that market leaders are created by a new set of rules.

Treacy and Wiersema published The Discipline of Market Leaders before the internet became such a force in commerce and business. Leveraging the world wide web to connect businesses and consumers has had a major impact on how business is done and likely the biggest impact on industry since the great industrial revolution. In the next chapter we will investigate how the internet has set up the foundation for new rules.

Chapter 2 – The Internet & E-commerce

Once, I participated in the Black Friday experience. One time and never again. I think it was circa 1988, even before the internet was a thing and a local mega-store, Nebraska Furniture Mart, had a special on a color TV that I thought was a good bargain. Maybe it was $300 or something, but good enough that I thought I should buy one. So, being the anxious shopper that I was, I set the alarm for 5:00 AM and, with drive time, arrived at the store around 5:45. When I pulled into the parking lot, I couldn't believe what I was seeing. The last time I saw that many tents was at Boy Scout Jamboree! Are you kidding me? People camped out all night? To save how much? Were they all there to purchase my TV? Darn!

Turns out, they had only allocated about 30 televisions at the advertised price and by the time I got into the store and found the line and saw about 50 campers already lined up, I was done, gone, and back home promising to never participate in Black Friday again!

I hate crowds. I loathe traffic jams. I detest malls. I can't cope with finding a parking spot in a crowded lot. I really don't like to shop, at least in the conventional sense. When e-commerce became a thing, for me, it was sent from heaven. I shop online whenever I can. Yes, according to Pew Research in 2000, I join 79% of my fellow Americans who do that which is up from 22%. In fact, I go out of my way to shop online during the Christmas season. I just don't have the patience to put up with the crowds and the nonsense.

The internet has likely become the most significant economic engine ever. Without the internet, we would, likely, still be in the industrial revolution. How many businesses are 100% dependent on the internet to function and offer their services? How many of you are connected? I am almost certain that anyone reading this is somehow connected to the internet. I can only think of kids younger than 8 and those maybe over 90 aren't "connected." And I might be underestimating that. Either way, you get the point.

The rise of e-commerce has taken the world by storm and notable companies such as Amazon, Alibaba, Netflix, Craigslist, and Google dominate their respective markets and without the internet, they wouldn't be in existence.

Okay, I am a male and I didn't inherit the "shopping gene" in my DNA. I would rather do almost anything than to go shopping. However, I like to buy things. I like new stuff. So, when I shop I have a couple of choices. I can do the old-fashioned method and figure out what store(s) I want to visit and see if they have what I am looking for. I am not one for browsing or window shopping. For me, when I go shopping, I have something in mind. Maybe it's not fully cemented in my head, but I have a general idea of what I need. Maybe it's a pair of pants, a shirt or even a pair of shoes. Or, maybe it's a hammer, or screw driver or a drill.

I'm not one to think about going to the mall and window shopping because I have a couple hours of free time.

In addition to getting in my car, fighting traffic, finding a reasonable parking spot and enduring the weather elements to get into a store, I must navigate the store to determine where the item is I wish to purchase. If I am shopping for clothes, I must hope they have a color I like and have my size in stock. Granted, the advantage of shopping for clothes in a store is I can try any item on to see if it fits. And I can get a better idea of the quality of the item. But, all too often my size isn't available. Or, it is available but not in the color I want. That causes me to go to yet another store to find my item.

If I am shopping for hardware, and I do prefer that, about 80% of the time I first find someone in a large box store and ask the whereabouts of the item I am seeking. All too often, not only can't I find the item I am seeking, I can't find help in the store to help me find my item and so I tend to waste too much time. My point is that shopping at a store, in my opinion, is a crap shoot. Sometimes it works out and sometimes it doesn't.

Either way, whenever I go to a store, I get the privilege of feeling and touching my item and even trying it on, but it takes far too much time. My wife always gets upset with me but when I go shopping for clothes, I buy in bulk. I should probably buy all my clothing at Costco, you know where they love to bundle in bulk, but they just have too limited of selections. If I go shopping for a new suit for example, I'm likely to buy two suits. Or, if I'm shopping for pants, likely to buy 2-3. Same thing with shirts. Why? Because for me shopping is such a hassle, I don't want to do it again soon.

One of the negatives of shopping in person is being able to compare prices. If I'm at Home Depot looking at drills, I ask myself what the price might be across the street at Lowe's. Home Depot and Lowes are located near each other for a very basic reason: the idea was first described by economist named Harold Hotelling in an academic paper entitled "Stability in Competition." in 1929. Also, a German Walter Christaller wrote a thesis known as the "Central Place Theory" that observed people who travel long distances are more likely to shop/live where there is convenience and ample supply of things they need. And yes, thank you Home Depot and Lowe's for locating your stores close to each other. At least I don't have to endure a long drive to check other prices. But what about Ace Hardware? Do you think they have a sale? What about Harbor Freight Sales? Do they have a drill that has any quality to it? The other thing I can't get from in-person shopping is feedback from other consumers.

Can you imagine walking up and down aisles, "Excuse me but do you own a Makita 360 brushless drill?". "If you do, has it been durable?" "What about the warranty?" "Look, I know you don't have time but here's my email address and if you could write up a review and email it to me that would be great.".

Of course, we don't do that. What we do is ask an attendant what they think of the product. It's like asking a waiter or waitress, "how's the tomato soup"? Of course, it's good. People working at the company may be on commission and they aren't going to tell you..." Look, if I were you, I would go over to Lowe's and get the Brand X as they are the only ones who sell it.". Or, a waitress isn't going to say, no the tomato soup is a bit watery, so you might want to try the salad". Yes, they might prefer one item over another, but they aren't exactly a neutral party that you can fully trust.

Once I have made my decision to purchase something, I get the pleasure of waiting in line to pay for it. How many of you have been to Walmart and seen 25 glimmering cashier stations at the front of the store but only two are open? Yes, those lines are frustrating, but at least they try and get you to buy some gum or other impulse item while you happen to be waiting. Why do stores invest in all that cash register hardware and waste so much space for something they never fully staff?

And what about the items that we all buy that won't fit in your vehicle? Yes, we all have great friends with pickup trucks, don't we? And we get the pleasure of returning to the store later to pick up those larger items. If I don't like coming to the store once, you can imagine what I think about a return trip just to haul my big loot home.

Now, let's review the online experience. In the comfort of my own home and likely in my pajamas, I can shop to my heart's content. I can search any item, read reviews, get feedback from other consumers and even ask questions that other consumers will answer about products. I can find out who is selling the product at the lowest possible price and can even shop for used items, refurbished by the factory.

I don't have to get in my car, fight traffic, hunt parking spots, hope they have what I am looking for, wait in cashier lines, carry my goodies to my car and drive back home. It's a great experience. However, I don't get the pleasure of trying something on or touching and feeling it for its quality. Thus, the clothes buying experience comes with greater risk. Also, there are times, especially with hardware-related items, that I need something right away, and I must make that trip to the store. And yes, there are times when I need to try something on.

Also, if you are shopping online you don't get the immediate gratification of immediate possession. You must wait a couple days. Well, in some markets, same-day is becoming the norm, but there are times when you have to trade-off the experience for immediate possession.

Do you remember when there were articles about how consumers would shop at Best Buy to test the quality of a television or other electronic gizmo only to not buy it there but go home and shop for the item they test online? Yeah, that happens, and I would say there just might be a correlation between the cost of an item and one's willingness to both shop in person to test the quality but then price becomes more important and shopping around online is typical.

So, does that mean every online merchant or e-commerce company is going to be phenomenally successful? Of course not. However, it's essential for nearly every company to have an online presence. You must have an online presence because consumers want to research and find you. But how you approach your online presence and experience can make or break you.

I will say this more than once: It's like a poker game. The ante is to have a website. You must have a web presence, if you want to play. However, just a website alone is not enough. The two most important elements of having a website are:

1) People need to know within 4 seconds what it is you do or what you sell. People are impatient and if on your home page, one cannot determine what you do or what you sell, they are gone and will not return. Keep your message simple and use 4th grade communication.

2) Your navigation is directly tied to the experience of your prospect or customer. Every key stroke counts! In other words, if you force your prospects or customers into visiting multiple screens, hitting multiple keys to engage you, they will ultimately find someone else that makes navigation easy, simple and fast. Remember, people are impatient and seconds count!

These two are critical points and are part a mathematical formula I call the *Hassle Quotient*. The less time and effort spent to navigate, purchase and check out are critical. I will point to many examples, but I cannot stress enough how important this element is. It is important for your customer or consumer to understand what you do, quickly and easily engage or purchase from you. It's that simple. However, as I will point out, the third element is what makes the dominant companies stand out. Yes, you can have a great experience and require little time and effort but if your prices aren't the best, you won't be dominant. You might be a good or great company, but you will not dominate. You cannot dominate by focusing on and nailing a single discipline. In today's world, you must do it all.

I will devote an entire chapter to Amazon, but they have mastered the formula known as the *Hassle Quotient*. While there are others, Amazon has mastered the *Hassle Quotient* and have leveraged it to be the dominant company they are today. While everyone likely knows what Amazon does, at its core, even someone dropping in from Mars would understand they sell things, lots of things. In moments, anyone could search for practically any durable good they are seeking. They might not fully understand that Amazon is a marketplace for many companies to promote their goods, but they would quickly understand that they can buy almost anything on Amazon.

Amazon has an amazing search engine, the ability to see how other consumers rate the product and even ask or see answers to common questions about the product. You can purchase items with one click, yes one click! They have as easy and simple return policy and with their Prime membership can get free two-day shipping. And, because they are a marketplace, and not just selling items they make or distribute, they create internal price competition that benefits the consumer. I think far too many overlook the fact that Amazon is a marketplace. You don't just see one item available via Amazon but that specific item might be offered by multiple vendors and thus create competition for price and customer service by multiple vendors. That is very important to keep pricing most competitive whereby most e-commerce companies sell their items and only one of each SKU (stock keeping unit) is available. Amazon is an amazing company and I will use them as a prime example of a company that uses unconventional thinking to dominate. They make it simple, easy, takes little time or effort and the experience is outstanding with feedback and questions, minimal clicks and highly competitive prices with free two-day shipping for many of their items.

There is a lot more to Amazon but it's as good as it gets for an online e-commerce experience and why they absolutely dominate.

Uber is another company that dominates their space. Google dominates their space. Facebook dominates their space. They all use a mathematical formula I call the *Hassle Quotient* as their overall strategy, though if you asked an executive they likely wouldn't say it in those terms, but it is true. Save your customer time, effort and money while giving them the best price value leads to market domination. They don't allow one element to be traded off for another. They could, but then they would take a step down to be a great or good company. Amazon *could* charge higher prices and still be a good company. Uber *could* make their mobile app a little more difficult to navigate and do fine. Google *could* make searching more difficult and be okay and Facebook *could* charge a subscription and likely be worthwhile.

I remember when I first heard about the internet, or the world-wide web. I admit I didn't really understand it. My first question was: "What is the difference between the internet and the world-wide web?" It was a very foggy concept to a person who didn't really know much about technology.

But then again, it would be ten years after graduating from college that I would be introduced to a personal computer. Heck, I was just getting used to the green screens.

You hear a lot of terms for this economic cycle we are in. Some call it the gig economy, others the platform economy, the networked economy, the sharing economy, the on-demand economy, the peer economy or the bottom up economy. You've probably heard these, and maybe other terms bandied about, often interchangeably, to describe how companies like Uber, Airbnb and Amazon, and countless others operate.

The trouble is, these terms are not interchangeable, and none of them accurately sums up the phenomenon they're trying to name. What is the phenomenon? Here's an attempt at an overall summary: *The restructuring of the traditional relationships between workers, resources, and customers made possible by digital systems for* **connecting** *them to one another with low transaction costs.*

The key term is "connecting". The internet has made it easy to connect one another to each other. It's a perfect vehicle for anyone selling a product or a service to connect to a broad audience very quickly, efficiently and cost-effectively.

I received a degree in marketing in the mid-1970's. Practically everything I learned from my marketing courses is now obsolete. The rules have changed. Can you imagine any company today operating without their own website? Have you ever heard of Constant Contact? Saleforce.com? Google, for goodness sake? When I was in school Spam was a canned meat (well something in a can anyway) and not unwanted emails that clog your inbox. Opt-in would have been a term more defined for the armed services than for subscribing to newsletters and email blasts.

Encyclopedias died, and Google thrives. We are all connected and now the dream vacation is one where you go somewhere and cannot be connected. Those places are harder to find, by the way. The adoption of the internet reminds me of when the transportation industry went from a regulated environment to a deregulated one. When the world became wired, many companies failed to recognize that it wasn't a fad, it was a trend and one that would radically change the world in so many ways.

Think about it for a moment. What would your day be like if the internet didn't exist? And it has only been commercialized just over 20 years. I can't even fathom what the next 20 years will bring. However, every day I read about the death of the retail store. I don't see travel agents on every corner any longer. No encyclopedia salesmen knock on my door. My mailbox contains mostly junk mail, no personal letters.

During the past 20 years or so we have gone from thinking about personal computers, to mobile devices and now on the cusp of artificial intelligence which will spawn an entirely new set of capabilities, companies and services.

One of my favorite athletes was Wayne Gretzky. During his prime, people wanted to know what made him so great. His answer was one that has stuck with me. Most people skate to where the puck is. I skate to where the puck is going to be. That has stuck with me and I often joke that I can't remember what I had for breakfast. By that I mean, I really don't care what happened yesterday or even earlier today. I care about what is about to happen.

I started a dot com logistics business back in 1999. I had a vision of creating a non-asset based less-than-truckload (LTL) carrier. I was going to utilize existing warehouses to perform the consolidation and de-consolidation activities during the off-hours that a warehouse works. I was going to use the internet as my means of connecting all the providers, from warehouses to small pick-up and delivery companies to our entire admin and operations team.

I basically wrote a business plan, a vision and was toying with it when one day I read an article in the Wall Street Journal that changed everything. On the front page of the Wall Street Journal there was an article about a 23-year-old MBA grad named Steve Rothschild who had founded furniture.com and venture capitalists in Silicon Valley were bidding against each other to fund his business. Steve was leveraging multiple VCs against each other to increase his valuation and get the best deal.

While I found the story interesting, what struck me was how a 23-year-old MBA student could know all there was to know about the furniture business. I had 20 years of experience in the transportation industry and thus my knowledge was surely worth something. That article spurred me to act and start a company we named freightpro.com. While I never got VCs in a bidding war, I did ultimately receive funding after proving that we could generate revenue. It took much longer and was much harder than I had originally anticipated (by the way, most everything takes more time and effort than one thinks). There were lots of bumps in the road and I have lots of stories but will save them for a later date.

What I will disclose is that the original business plan never played out. We needed significant shipments to be able to consolidate and provide competitive transit time service and so the shipments we did secure, were brokered to LTL carriers. However, there was value in that as we leveraged the internet to engage shippers in a simplified and easy way. We also learned there was significant value in providing customized logistics solutions to shippers and again, using the internet and our customized application to serve them. Most any entrepreneur will tell you that you must adapt to changing conditions and what you originally thought would work, may indeed not work and you must adjust.

We adjusted, and the company ultimately generated $25 million in sales after 5 years and was Earnings Before Interest Taxes Depreciation and Amortization (EBITDA) positive until we lost our biggest customer. Unfortunately, we ended up with an account that was 70% of our revenue and we were saving them a lot of money and we were making a lot of money until they had a management change and decided to go in a new direction. It was one of the most painful, yet valuable lessons I ever learned. I knew better than to allow a single customer to bring us down, but it wasn't planned, it just happened. If there is any solace at all, we lasted far longer than furniture.com did.

After raising $13 million in their Series A round, furniture.com was successful in raising a total of $50 million in three rounds. In 2000, just two years after launching, they attempted an IPO and due to the dot.com crash, pulled the offering before going public. It wasn't long after that, due to mounting losses, they shut the doors.

The best thing to come out of this entire experience was learning how technology enables innovation, especially given the resources available through the internet. I distinctly recall that during my freightpro.com days, a start-up was being hammered by the press. It was a company burning through millions of dollars and no clear path to profit and the founder and CEO was being tortured by the business press. This CEO persevered and was relentless in his quest to change the way business was done, using the internet as the fundamental building block to his business. I will devote an entire chapter to Jeff Bezos and Amazon, but it has worked out quite well.

Another important lesson is that timing is everything. During the early days of the internet and e-commerce, a company named Webvan was making a splash. They were making a splash due to the amount of money being invested in them and the amount of cash burn they experienced. It was all about the home delivery of groceries. They didn't survive. They were ahead of their time as today, many are offering such a service and there is great demand for it. Regardless of business model, it is important to put the customer first, save them time, effort and money while giving them a better experience than what they currently enjoy.

In my opinion, a company's priority and goals should be centered on their customer and religiously figuring out ways to save them time, save them effort, save them money and at the same time, delivering the very best user experience possible. That should be the mission of every company and it is for those that dominate and those that leapfrog their competition.

Without question, the internet has allowed for new rules of business and particularly new ways to engage customers. Next, we are going to evaluate the formula that dominant companies are using, whether they know it or not, and the internet plays a very key role in that formula. In fact, a few dominant companies rely 100% on the internet for their existence.

Chapter 3 – The *Hassle Quotient* Formula

I am not a psychologist though I did take one course in college. However, I know a couple of deep secrets about you, each of you. What I know about you is exactly what the most successful companies know about you. Dominant companies center their universe around you, the customer, and they know these things and more. The "more" they learn by asking you. That's right. They ask. They don't presume or think, they ask. In today's new, internet-centric economy, the leading companies don't think internally, they think externally. Essentially, dominant companies, think about the customer first and then engineer backward so that everything they do meets the needs, and strive to surpass the needs and desires of the customer.

Dominant companies don't sit around the boardroom and strategize whether they should be an operationally excellent, customer intimate or product-centric company, they focus on customer need and then engineer the operations to be exceedingly efficient for the customer's benefit, develop customer services processes that endear customers to them and, if they have products (not a service company) they support those products, so customers become disciples and/or zealots of the company.

It's too easy for a company to say they put the customer first. I've never known a company to say, "we don't care about the customer." That wouldn't be a good look. However, most companies that *say* they put the customer first rarely practice that. There are typically too many pressures facing companies to practice putting the customer first. The biggest pressure is financial results. Companies tend to have shareholders and most companies put the shareholders before the customer and shareholders want returns on equity and financial growth. So, all too often, to get financial results, focus goes to costs, productivity and sales.

Wait, I said sales. Don't confuse increasing sales to placing the customer at the top of the focus chain. Most companies think they need better sales people, more productive sales people and better Customer Relationship Management Systems. Sales needs to learn how to close more business! Sales must beat the competition and maybe all they need are promotions or discounts to get their numbers up. Anyone who has been in sales knows the drill. Maybe the company rolls out new products or services. That will increase sales. Maybe an increase in advertising, or digital marketing!

There's a lot that goes into putting the customer first, after all, companies are complex mechanisms and must master many disciplines to operate successfully. Do all functions within a company have to put the customer first? Does the accounting department have to put the customer first? Yes, for those parts of accounting that touch the customer. It's a culture that must be adopted. It's probably easier to adopt a culture of putting the customer first and working backward from the onset of the company than it is to re-engineer that culture. Change is hard in a company and placing the customer first goes well beyond talk. It's more than a reorganization, or simply naming a Chief Customer Officer. This culture must be embraced at the top. The CEO and the Board of Directors must adopt this customer-centric culture, be brave, overcome fear and not waver as external financial pressures will present themselves, but over the long term, putting customers first and working toward being a dominant company will result in the financial benefits everyone is seeking, it's just sometimes counter-intuitive.

To become a dominant company, you must focus on the customer first and engineer backward. You also must know a lot about your customers, or customer personalities and psychology. You must understand some of the underlying behaviors we, as humans, have. A couple stand out.

As humans, we are naturally lazy, or said another way, we want things to be easy. We prefer easy to hard. Do you remember when Staples came out with the Easy Button advertising campaign. That is us. We all want that button and want it to work. As you read this some of you might not react kindly to this notion. You are hard-working and spend countless hours on your job. Some of you will outright reject that notion. I know you don't want to hear that, nor do you want to admit it, but it is true. Let me prove it to you. Let's say you can buy a barbeque grill at the store. It comes assembled, or you can buy it in pieces and assemble it yourself but it's the same price either way. Me? I know I am going to take the assembled version. After all, I'm not the type that says, "gee I have a bunch of time to kill, sure would be a good way to spend an afternoon assembling a BBQ grill that I didn't have to put together." It's a different decision if the grill cost $40 more for assembly.

Or, let's say you buy a new bedroom set at the furniture store and they will deliver it for free, or of course, you can arrange to pick it up. Okay, I know my neighbor Ted has that pickup truck and he's dying to have me ask if I can borrow it. But does he have rope and tie downs? Unless you have a lot of time to kill and enjoy asking and driving Ted's truck, you know the answer. Heck yes, it's easier for me to have them deliver it.

Let's say the lawn needs mowing or the dishes need washed. What if there were absolutely no consequences to the lawn not being mowed or the dishes not being washed? If there were absolutely no consequences such as the grass growing more and making the job harder each day, or being unsightly and neighbors giving you "the look", would you rather mow the lawn or sit and watch TV? I know many of you are saying you absolutely would go mow the lawn.

My final example and one that just might resonate with you. Have you ever gone to a fast food restaurant and the drive through is backed up twenty cars? Yet, you look at the parking lot and only see a couple of parked cars. People will wait in their cars for twice as long as it would take to park and walk into the restaurant and order from the counter. It's true and if you don't believe me, check out a McDonald's restaurant next time you are near one. I know you don't do this, but others do, right? Yes, it can take a lot longer to go through a drive-through, even a bank drive-through then to

49

park and walk in and do your business at the counter. However, it is so much easier to sit in one's car and wait for the line to move along. After all, it's probably 100 steps to go in and come back out, plus of course the hassle and effort of parking and locking one's car.

However, human nature is to take the path of least resistance. Let's take another example. You must go to the store and it's 3 blocks away. You can walk, you can ride your bike, or you can take your car. There are consequences to each. If you walk, it takes the most amount of time and then you must carry the groceries back to your place. If you ride the bike, it's a bit quicker but you need to secure your bike at the store and then limit your groceries due to the capacity of the bike. The car is the fastest and can haul the most groceries. And, oh by the way, the method that requires you to exert the least amount of physical effort is to take the car.

Let's not confuse boredom for not being lazy. Again, that is a consequence. Because of me being bored, guess I'll go wash those dishes. If all things were equal and there were zero consequences, people would opt to do nothing. We prefer easy to hard. We all want the real Staples button. Companies know this about us. They don't come out with products that make our lives hard or more difficult, or at least shouldn't.

Number two. As humans, we are all impatient. Many talk about the young generation whether they be called millennials or Gen Xers, and how they have this "want it now" attitude. We are all that way. Admit it, if all things were equal, we want it now. Let me give you an example. Let's say a friend offered you $100 cash with no strings attached. None! He asks if you want the $100 now or they can give it to you 3 days from now. You are going to take the $100 now as there aren't any consequences. In fact, you might be afraid the deal will fall apart, and your friend change his mind, so you absolutely want it now.

I don't know if I came up with this or copied it, but one of my favorite quotes is "If I wanted it tomorrow, I would ask for it tomorrow." Another quote I love is from Carrier Fisher who once said, "Instant gratification takes too long."

According to CNN, the total household debt in the U.S. is a staggering $12.5 trillion, yes with a "T". The all-time high household debt was 2008 which was just before the meltdown caused by the mortgage crisis. There was a commercial that was one of my favorites. It showed a man in front of his lovely house in the suburbs with a well-maintained lawn, two cars and a boat in the drive way and mentioning all his assets. He states he has this new home, two cars, a big family and a boat. "How do I do it? I'm in debt up to my eyeballs." Seriously, with the emergence of the credit card, you see something, you buy it. You don't have to save for it, you pay for it later. Want to take that great vacation? No money? No problem.

I'm as guilty as anyone but I know my parents didn't do that. Maybe it's because they grew up during the Great Depression and had very little and what they did have treasured it. My parents saved for it and then purchased it.

We don't do that anymore. And guess what? Leading companies know we aren't patient and understand the psychology to get us to buy now. Companies use peer pressure to make you think that everyone is purchasing this or doing that, and why not you? It's like when a teenager tells their parents that "Joey's parents are letting him....." Fill in the blank.

Maybe you are a fan of HGTV. How many shows are there about flipping houses? You see, house flippers understand that buyers would rather purchase a completed and updated house than to buy a project and spend a lot of time and effort to fix it up themselves. House flippers leverage the psychology that we want things now and we are basically lazy. They generate huge profits leveraging that set of human behaviors.

Or even simpler, when you want to sell your house, you are well-advised to maybe put a fresh coat of paint on a few walls, clean carpets, perhaps de-clutter some areas and do a deep cleaning. Potential buyers are less likely to purchase something that needs immediate work, or if they are, they are going to buy at a significant discount. Home buyers suspect that if they can see something not to their liking, there is likely a lot more that they cannot see. "Honey, the house needs painting. I'll bet they haven't cleaned their air ducts either and maybe there is mold behind the bathroom walls."

These two behaviors combined make for a powerful combination for companies that understand them and can cater to our need for get it now and make it easy for customers as they don't want to exert much effort. In fact, the internet and buying on-line is all about giving immediate gratification and leveraging our natural laziness by encouraging us to hit a few keystrokes. Easy and immediate is what it is all about.

Another behavior that we consumers demonstrate, and have for years, is that everyone enjoys a bargain. Even billionaires enjoy bargains and will brag about the deal they got on their latest helicopter or private jet.

The most successful companies in today's economy use a mathematical formula to take advantage of our behavioral tendencies. Companies like Amazon, Uber, Airbnb, Netflix, Facebook, Google and others deploy this formula with great success. Dominant companies use this formula almost like Coca Cola or Kentucky Fried Chicken uses and protects their secret formula. However, if you were to open the vaults at Amazon or Uber for example, there wouldn't be a formula written down and if you asked them to name their formula, they might call it something else. I call it the *Hassle Quotient* as I believe it is mathematical and measurable.

The Hassle Quotient is Mathematical and Measurable

There are many companies who don't understand the formula and are ripe to be transformed. Recently, at a conference, Terry Jones, the founder of Travelocity made a profound statement. If you are an existing company and new competitors are formed to change your industry or business model, you would call that disruption. You have been disrupted is the context. If you are the one disrupting, you would call it innovation. I like that as I really don't like the term disruption, when a company or an industry is put out of business by a better user experience, that is disruptive. But the companies that are most successful in today's economy don't have a strategy to disrupt anything. They have a strategy to make it easier, faster and simpler for customers to engage them than their competitors. That is transformation.

Transformative companies in today's economy are finding ways to make it easier for customers to engage them, have them spend less time and effort than current options, provide the best price or cost and excel with a superior overall customer experience. That is the formula!

I will be giving you multiple examples of this theory and formula but the ultimate key for a successful company in today's environment is to make it less of a hassle for a customer to do business with you than anyone else or any other option. The mathematical formula is called the Hassle Quotient. The lower your Hassle Quotient (HQ), the more likely you are to be a dominant company. However, it is not easy to accomplish all components of the formula. In other words, it is very difficult to allow your customers to engage you with little time and effort, have the lowest prices and provide the best user experience. It's those last two that are most difficult, and most companies use a trade-off. They give the lowest price, but the user experience is not ideal or give the very best user experience, but their prices reflect the experience.

Here is the formula:

$$\text{Hassle Quotient} = \frac{(\text{Time} + \text{Effort}) + \text{Cost}}{\text{User Experience}}$$

I like to express the *Hassle Quotient* (HQ) in terms of an actual mathematical equation. I believe the lower the number and subsequent HQ, the better for the customer. That would mean that a low number for the numerator would be good. A score of 1 for time would be a good score. Conversely, the customer should rate the denominator, or customer experience as good, with a high number.

You have the option of asking customers to rate both numerator and denominator either way, but one must be rated highly with a low number and the other with a high number. They should not be the same.

For my examples, I prefer to use a low numerator as a good experience when it comes to time, effort and price and use a high number when a customer rates the overall customer experience. That means the lower the Hassle Quotient, the better. It means it's less of a hassle and ultimately more convenient. The higher the HQ, the less likely a customer is going to have a great experience.

A simple way to express the Hassle Quotient Formula could be this

$$\text{Hassle Quotient} = \frac{\text{Convenience} + \text{Cost}}{\text{User Experience}}$$

Keep in mind that this formula is based upon what your customers think. It doesn't matter what you, the company think. You need to ask the customer to rate the amount of time and effort they spend to engage your company compared to competitors. Ask how they compare your prices to competitors and ask them to compare their overall customer experience to your competitors. Then you can compare your HQ to that of your overall competitive landscape.

Now, the elements of this quotient are subjective. One must understand their customer to really tailor their offering to their targets. There is a saying that the two most precious commodities are time and money. An old joke amongst men is that you could include hair, but we'll stick to time and money. Personally, I think the most precious commodity is time. I don't have enough of it and many I interact with tell me the same thing. It's funny though, with the innovation of apps, many are developed to save us time. So, what do we do? We don't enjoy the added time afforded us by those apps, we tend to cram in more activity in that time. We try and get more done! We are crammers!

Under this assumption, you could break the entire population into one of those two categories and cater to them. There is a correlation between time and money. Those with the most money tend to have the least amount of time and those with the most time are likely to have less money. In other words, there are people who will spend an inordinate amount of time to save the proverbial dollar. On the other hand, there are those who value their time so much, will spend whatever it takes to save time. Thus, convenience-oriented businesses, cater to those and can charge a premium.

A convenience store, for example, sells some grocery items at a premium to what you can buy that product from in a full-scale grocery store. However, it takes more time to shop in a grocery store if all you need is a can of cola. That's the idea. On the other side of the spectrum, there are many people who scour weekly ads, clip coupons and drive around town to multiple stores to get the very best deal. They don't care how long it takes, if they get the very best deal and save money. Time isn't as important to them, saving money is.

Pricing format is part of the experience. Variable pricing where the customer doesn't know the price up front is a terrible experience. Nickel and diming on top of a base price is an awful experience. You and me, as consumers, want to know the price or cost up front, or have a very solid range. So, when I use the term "cost" I am referring to math or a quantifiable number that can be compared to another price or cost. If I can get a one-hour massage for $50 at Brand A and it costs $65 at Brand B, that is what I am speaking about.

It's very easy for a service business to charge on a per unit basis that doesn't allow the consumer to understand the full cost up front. Attorneys are a great example. They charge per hour and you have no clue how many hours they need and then get surprised on how many hours it takes.

Early in my career I engaged a warehouse company to store goods, fulfill orders and accept new inventory from time-to-time. The pricing structure was variable and, on a per-pallet basis, something like $5 per pallet to receive, $5 per pallet to ship and $10 per pallet per month for storage and $5 if a pallet was stored less than one month. The very first invoice I received contained costs for creating and mailing the invoice I received. I actually was charged for copying the invoice and paid for the bloody stamp they used. Granted, these costs were a tiny fraction of the total, but it left a lasting bad impression on me and an example of "nickel and diming." Airlines are famous for nickel and diming as well, some more than others.

A few of you may be old enough to remember the days of telephone land lines. Yes, most houses had them and I remember that long distance was less expensive during nights and weekends and we would wait until the weekends to call relatives to get the cheaper rate. We, or at least I, had no idea what the rate was, but we knew it was less expensive. Now of course, very few people have a land line and we have flat rates with our cellular service provider with some built-in limits on data and talk time with some plans.

Also, back in the day, car rental companies imposed a mileage fee and they varied by car type and whether it was weekend or week day driving. Now, all car rental companies have unlimited miles even though some might drive 400 miles per day and others 40, the charges are the same. Granted, with both cell phones and car rentals, there are many additional fees and surcharges, but most of those are the results of governments, typically local, imposing taxes to build their revenues.

Let's look at each element in the Hassle Quotient formula.

Time & Effort – These two values are highly related. If something takes a lot of effort, it is likely going to take a lot of time. It takes a lot of time to mow my grass and it's a good-sized effort. If I am going to the mall, it takes a lot of time and effort. I must get in my car, travel to the mall, find a parking spot (ugh!), walk into the mall, figure out the location of the store I need to visit, walk to the store, shop, stand in line to pay, walk back to my car (hope I can find it), drive home. There are a couple examples of where it takes a lot of time, but not so much effort. You ever been to the DMV? Not so much effort but the time? Oh my. But the government isn't a competitive business and so you have no options. Many doctors' offices and emergency rooms take a lot of time but not a lot of effort.

An example of where effort can be more than time is moving. If you and your buddy decide to pack and move your furnishings, it takes a lot of effort. An option is to hire two people to move your furnishings. It likely will take the same amount of time, but a lot less effort.

Pretty much though, time and effort go together. Let me give you a perfect example of time and effort. Do you know which search engine is the 2nd most popular search engine? Google dominates that space but the 2nd most popular search engine might surprise you. It's YouTube. That's right, YouTube. YouTube was created in 2005 and by 2006 had 100 million views per day. By 2010, they had 2 billion views per day and became the 3rd most popular website on the internet.

What gives? Why do you think YouTube is so wildly successful? I haven't polled all 2 billion users each day, but I suspect that it is so popular because it's easy and it tells us the story. We don't have to read! Reading is harder than someone telling me the same thing, or even demonstrating something to me. If I must read illustrations or instructions, it's much easier for me to comprehend via a video. Yes, I can find everything I need by using Google, but it's much easier and takes a lot less effort for someone to show me. I believe YouTube is a leading indicator that, when given a choice, we humans prefer to spend less time and exert less effort performing a task.

Cost – Let's examine IKEA. The reason I am willing to spend so much time, exert so much effort and pore through complicated instructions is the cost is highly preferential to the other options at my disposal. So, cost or price depending upon point of view, is significantly tied to the other factors.

If something takes a lot of time, a lot of effort, is complicated AND expensive, that is about the worst experience I can think of. On the other hand, if I don't have to spend much time and effort and is straight-forward, I don't mind paying a higher price.

User Experience – This one is very subjective. What does the consumer think about the experience? Many companies and brands sell and promote their experience. When I think Marriott compared to Super 8, I get a much better experience. I especially love those Marriott beds. But, I'm going to pay double or triple the price for a night's stay. Am I buying an experience or a night's stay?

I believe customer experience has a lot of factors depending upon if it is a brick and mortar or online experience:

Brick and Mortar

- Cleanliness
- Good lighting
- Friendly staff
- Available staff
- Organized store
- Sufficient check out resources
- Sufficient and convenient parking

Online

- Understanding of what you do on landing page

- Easy search feature
- Minimal key strokes
- Minimal page view
- Easy registration
- Option out of marketing emails or spam
- Rated products and services
- Easy to navigate and understand

Recently in Gary's Greeting, Southwest's CEO talked about improving the customer experience for Southwest fliers. He said, "When we think about the customer experience, we don't simply mean customer service. Sure, that's part of it, but we think of the experience as our relationship with you from the time you visit our website or call us to when you arrive at your destination – and all points in between." He points out that customer experience involves every touch point, including their frequent flier program. Southwest boasts about their unlimited reward seats and imposes no blackout dates and points don't expire.

I'm a big fan of Southwest largely due to not liking being nickel and dimed. I loved their advertisement where they poked fun at their competitors by having coin slots for access to the overhead luggage compartment, to recline the seat and even to get access to the lavatory. We will talk about nickel and diming later, but consumers prefer an all-inclusive price and they detest unknown surprises. I know I for one, hate the fine print so to speak.

Even though, as humans, we share in the traits of laziness or wanting things easy and we are basically impatient, we all have differing opinions as to customer experience and we all value money differently.

For example, I have a friend who lives in a smaller town that has three grocery stores. She would cut coupons out of the local paper for each store and drive to each looking for the very best bargain she could find for products that were on sale. It really didn't matter to her what she needed, she knew that at some point in time, she would need mustard, so might as well buy it on sale and stock it until her supply runs out. She would spend hours shopping in this manner. Did she save the most amount of money? You bet she did? Was it a hassle? You bet it was. In that case, she simply didn't put the value on her time that I might.

Bargain hunters will go to great length to save a buck. I can't fault them, but their value system is different than mine. I value my time very highly and thus, while I like a bargain, I am not going to go to extremes with my precious time to save a few cents here and there.

Aldi's is a great example of a store that offers exceptional value, but they make each customer go through more effort than I want to exert. First, you need to pay a deposit of $.25 just to use a shopping cart. Next, you won't find many brand names, but you will find great prices. You also won't find every item that the larger grocery stores will carry. There is no butcher shop, no deli nor no prepared food. And you best bring your own bags or buy them from Aldi. They are all about catering to the thrifty and those willing to exert more effort to save money. Interestingly, Aldi's slight produce section does offer organic fruits and vegetables and at low prices, so that is a good value for many shoppers.

However, as I will prove, just because a company chooses to offer low prices doesn't necessarily mean they have to force customers into extra time, effort and complexity and overall provide a terrible customer experience. In fact, the real winners are those who understand that humans want to minimize time and effort, spend as little as possible and enjoy a superior experience. If you can do it all, you create a tremendous competitive advantage.

However, many companies understand that by minimizing time, minimizing effort, making it simple and providing the best experience possible, they can demand and get a premium, and do. Nordstrom's comes to mind for being in that category. Many e-commerce companies are in that category. Many fine dining establishments fall here too. I will discuss an industry that doesn't understand this formula and derive price solely based on their cost. They are losing billions of dollars of revenue and millions of dollars of profit by not understanding the hassle quotient formula and how to leverage a market-based price by giving customers the very best experience and minimizing the hassle.

One can assign numbers to come up with a real formula. But to do this right way, customers should assign the numbers. Have customers assign a number between 1-10 in all categories, with 10 being the worst and 1 being the best. From there, you simply add up and do the math. The lower the number the better.

Examples:

Let me provide you some examples on how the formula works and compute a few *Hassle Quotients*. Remember, the value I place on the variables is my personal feelings and I may value my time more, or less, than anyone else. I may rate the experience differently than others. That is one of the strongest points I will make about companies. It doesn't matter what the company *thinks* about the experience they provide, the amount of time and effort it takes someone to engage the customer and how simple it is to do business with them. It's all about how a company's customers and consumers in general think about those things.

If you aren't constantly taking the pulse of your customers and acting on what they are telling you, then you deserve your company's outcome. Just because sales and profits are improving doesn't mean a competitor isn't scheming how to change the rules of the game and make you obsolete. I'll make that point later when we discuss Uber and how it has transformed the taxi business. Anyone want to buy a cab company? I didn't think so. You know your competitors and you should be constantly taking the pulse of your customers on how you are compared with your competitors on time and effort to do business with you, how simple it is to engage you, what their overall experience is and how they rate you on your price and charges. I promise you that the lower your *Hassle Quotient*, the higher your customer satisfaction, the higher your sales and the higher your profit. You can correlate how much you charge based on these factors.

Companies will ultimately have to choose the customer segment they are seeking. For example, it's okay to cater to the budget shopper who values price over experience. It's also an acceptable strategy to cater to those who are willing to pay a higher price but want the very best experience. Regardless of which path a company chooses, ensure that you maximize the experience, minimize the time and effort it takes and how complicated you make it for a consumer.

Let me give you the examples with companies everyone knows. Again, these are how I personally assess the companies based on my own personal experiences and the value system I have for time, simplicity, price and overall experience. You might value them differently.

McDonalds

Ah, the golden arches where billions and billions are sold. I'm old enough to remember when they had an actual tally of hamburgers sold and posted it on their sign. I guess they got tired of changing the sign all the time and said the heck with that and went with the billions and billions. McDonalds does a lot of things right and have had their share of wrongs. However, there likely isn't anyone reading this who hasn't been a customer at some point.

One of my professors in college once said that McDonalds is the cornerstone for consistent mediocrity. Consistent in that a Big Mac in Hong Kong should taste like a Big Mac in Chicago. Many chains have tried to copy McDonalds and put a slight twist on it. After all, who doesn't want to copy billions and billions. Wendy's is a notable competitor and promote their burgers as meat that has never been frozen. Plus, they provide square patties and their process makes it very easy to customize one's order. Burger King took a jab at McDonalds and their frying of the burger by offering flame broiled burgers, seemingly like when you cook burgers on your grill in the backyard.

So, let's look at each variable in the formula:

- Time and Effort – I rate McDonalds highly compared to their competitors especially because there seems to be a McDonalds on almost every corner. In some cases, you will find McDonalds within a mile of each other. Also, they really have perfected the drive through process. They now typically have 2 lanes and a separate window for payment, separate for food pick up and even dedicated parking slots if your order requires extra time. Even if I go inside, they seem to have ample help behind the counter and I can get my food relatively quickly
- Price – McDonalds does not cater to the food connoisseur. Rather they cater to those who want a fast dining experience at a very reasonable cost. They

have a value menu featuring many items for a dollar. Most importantly, in my opinion, they provide real value on drinks. One can buy a large drink for a dollar where most competitors are near or more than double that price.

- User Experience – I think the food is very middle of the road. The burgers are okay, and I prefer Wendy's and Burger King's burgers to McDonalds. And don't get me started about In and Out Burger…yum. However, McDonalds does a nice job of delivering a great kid experience with its Happy Meal and many have built-in playgrounds. Many McDonalds have upped the ante with a better line of coffees and have WIFI. They lack comfort in their seating and it is a sterile environment, but they are looking to turn the seats quickly so that is somewhat by design.

$$Hassle\ Quotient\ (.75) = \frac{Time + Effort\ (2) + Price\ (1)}{User\ Experience\ (4)}$$

Home Depot

Since 1979, Home Depot has been servicing both the do-it-yourself home improvement and repairman to the professional contractor. They put together a super store to cater to consumers who used to shop at lumber yards, hardware stores, appliance stores, lawn and garden stores, carpet and flooring stores and much more. Lowe's, their major competitor, started just after world war II, but I don't recognize anything significantly difference between the two, except one has orange in its color schemes and one has blue. I assume the true professional contractor has and can identify differences, but for this purpose, they are like twins.

Home Depot is slightly larger than Lowes at $88.5 billion in revenue so I'm using them for this example. As you can tell from my description, Home Depot made it much simpler and more convenient by combining multiple home improvement categories under one roof. Who wants to shop multiple stores when doing a project when you can find whatever you need under one roof?

Again, this is my personal impression and rating of the variables that go into determining the hassle quotient.

- Time and Effort – For sure, there aren't as many Home Depot locations as there are McDonalds and they are in larger cities where the population will support them, but generally, for the size of store, they are relatively convenient. While it doesn't take a large amount of time for me to get to the store, once inside, is a different story. Being so large, it can take a lot of time to find the product you might be seeking. And, my biggest issue with this kind of superstore is they don't have enough help to direct me and answer questions which expands the amount of time I spend in the store.
- Price – Because they buy in such volume, typically I find Home Depot to be a better option than my local hardware store. Big ticket items are more expensive

at the local hardware store, but at my local hardware store I can purchase a single bolt or screw. At Home Depot I am forced into buying bulk items or pre-packaged to where I buy a dozen screws or bolts when I only need one. Then they sit on my workbench and maybe, just maybe, I will need that very screw sometime in the future.

- User Experience – I must rate the user experience just middle-of-the-road. While I typically have success finding an option for my needs at Home Depot, it takes time to drive there, find parking, find the items I need, get the quantity I really want and then find a cashier without a huge line. Like many, Home Depot now has self-checkout lanes. Certain items, however, just aren't conducive to self-checkout such as lumber or pipe which might not have bar codes on them.

I didn't realize that Home Depot and Lowe's have a remarkable feature on their mobile app. If you know the store you want to visit, you can look it up on their mobile app and it will tell you the exact location, aisle and bin location and even the number of items in stock. I tried it and it was awesome. However, the number of units wasn't correct but I saved a lot of time hunting down someone who knew where tarp clips were. Great experience and saved me a lot of time. Are you reading this Walmart, Target and you other "big box" retailers?

$$Hassle\ Quotient\ (1.6) = \frac{Time + Effort\ (6) + Price\ (2)}{User\ Experience\ (5)}$$

Wal-Mart

America's Superstore where everyday low prices offer you savings. Walmart is an American staple and the largest retailer in the world, not counting Amazon, at $485 billion in 2016. I want to specifically discuss the retail store and not their on-line business that competes with Amazon.

I remember the days when Walmart would come into a small town and practically wipe out the mom and pop shops on Main street. They have tremendous buying power and are expert logisticians and I claim they act more like a logistics company that sells stuff than a standard retailer. I can't imagine anyone who hasn't been to a Walmart. We all have our opinions of Walmart and I am no exception. Clearly, they are price leaders and cater to the budget-conscious crowd.

So, let me give you my view on how they stack up on the Hassle Quotient.

- Time and Effort – Their stores number somewhere between McDonalds and Home Depot. They do target smaller and mid-sized towns, unlike Home Depot because they sell every day consumer goods, including groceries in their Super Centers. Finding and driving to a Walmart isn't a problem. Finding a parking spot is. Walmart stores are popular and crowded. And, maybe it's my lack of knowledge, but it seems to me that every Walmart is laid out differently. I must get my bearings and then roam to find the department I need and the product. Also, Walmart frequently changes the products they sell. What you might find one trip, you might not find again. If I cannot find what I am seeking, it takes effort to find a clerk far too many times.

- Price – The Walmart brand is known for price leadership. Everything about them leads to their value proposition. Everyday low prices and Roll Back America are two popular slogans that Walmart coined and use frequently. While they may not have the lowest price on an item on a particular day, I trust Walmart to be the price leader on a more consistent basis than anyone else.

- User Experience – My personal belief is that Walmart trades off price and value over experience. As stated previously, typically hard to find a decent parking space, employees who can help direct someone are few and far between, stores are often cluttered, you meet very interesting people while shopping, sometimes the quality of goods isn't top-of-the-line and my biggest complaint is, although they might have 25 registers, they only man 10% of them. I know I am going to be in a long line when shopping at Walmart. Even their self-checkout lines are busy. My experience would be far superior if I could get through checkout quickly. Interestingly, Walmart is experimenting with multiple ways of improving the experience of the online shopper. They are creating special pickup points, lanes and parking spots for those who order online and simply want to drop by and pick their items up. It's partly an answer to Amazon, but maybe a much-needed sign of understanding how improving their user experience can gain them business.

Recently I saw a Facebook post by someone who said; "If I wanted to check myself out at Walmart, I would stay at home and shop Amazon."

$$Hassle\ Quotient\ (4.0) = \frac{Time + Effort\ (7) + Price\ (1)}{User\ Experience\ (2)}$$

So, if Walmart has the highest hassle quotient of all my examples, why are they the largest company of those compared? Obviously, people like Walmart proven by their nearly $500 billion in sales each year. You see, it's a trade-off. People are willing to trade off the user experience for low pricing. I'm no different on some things. Would I like to eat lunch each day at Ruth Chris? I get a great user experience, but my entire food budget would be out the window and I don't have the time it takes to make a reservation, be waited on, and take an hour or more for lunch. It's a trade-off.

Now, imagine if Walmart focused on their number one deficiency, the user experience. What if the greeter, instead of saying "Welcome to Walmart", they said "What can I help you find?" What if each store was laid out exactly the same, so we knew exactly where we needed to go within the store? What if they had a drive through for those who ordered online and didn't have to park? What if they used their big data to understand the demand of cashiers so that no one waited in line more than 2 minutes? What if they had enough associates in each department to pro-actively sell items? Shouldn't they be like a fast food restaurant and try and turn seats or shoppers faster? Shouldn't they encourage associates to get us to buy more on each visit? What if they had less clutter? What if they more consistently carried the same items in all the stores?

Sure, it might cost a bit higher, but Walmart is recognizing that paying their associates minimum wage is inhibiting their ability to attract and retain good employees. They are absorbing that cost and yet maintaining low prices, at least when compared to their competitors.

The key point for any company is to understand where you are deficient and increasing your Hassle Quotient score determined by a company's target customer. Understand that your customers really want it all and you, as a company, should do all you can to constantly lower your hassle, increase convenience while minimizing price.

Let's face it, people have differing behaviors. One might be driven to get the very best deal possible regardless of the amount of time and effort it takes and really don't care about the experience. Another, cares all about the user experience. I know someone that scours the weekly grocery ads, clips all the coupons for all the stores and then treks around to each store and purchases those items that are on sale and especially have coupons that lower their price below normal. She will buy items she doesn't currently need, and stocks them for when she might run out. If paper towels are on sale with a $2 coupon when you buy the "super pack", she is going to buy them and store them so that when she runs out of her current supply, they are there. Then she drives across town to another store for the toilet paper as they have the deal of the week on that item.

Do you know why malls are failing? I believe malls have a much higher *Hassle Quotient* than other retail outlets. I think the original premise was that by combining multiple retailers under a common roof, it would be easier for the consumer to shop and purchase multiple types of items with a single trip. Yes, some merit there, but parking is a nightmare, walking miles to accomplish one's objectives is time-consuming, carrying goods around requires effort, and pricing is all over the board, dependent upon the retailer selected. E-commerce companies, like Amazon, have huge appeal when comparing the *Hassle Quotient* to the mall, in my opinion.

There are thousands of start-ups that pop up each year. Many are now founded on the premise that their technology platform makes someone's lives easier. I know from a trucking perspective, many are attempting to use mobile applications to eliminate a layer in a typical transaction. It is very common in the truckload industry to use a broker given the high fragmentation of the capacity in the truckload industry. Many people think that by creating a mobile app to directly connect shippers and carriers together, the experience would take less time, less effort and price be more competitive by cutting out a layer. What they haven't figured out is the user experience, especially on the shipper side. Shippers don't have time to engage carriers directly and especially to vet and qualify the prospective carrier for the proper authority, insurance and then coordinate all the activity required to coordinate the pickup and delivery of loads. These "technology" startups have focused on only one side of the buyer/seller relationship and surmised that if they can save money for the shipper, all would be good.

Just deploying a mobile app isn't necessarily the answer. If a mobile app helps customers save time and effort while maximizing the customer's user experience is the outcome, then yes, that strategy makes perfect sense.

We are going to examine the real reason why Amazon is changing the way business is done and why they are a dominant company. They are the poster child for minimizing the *Hassle Quotient* for shoppers of all kind.

Chapter 4 - Amazon

I can't go into details about Amazon without first talking about e-commerce, in general, and how it has absolutely reshaped the buying habits of consumers. E-commerce is the absolute best example of how to minimize the hassle quotient by reducing the amount of time and effort it takes a consumer to shop and buy something. The online experience, for so many, is a better user experience in addition to saving huge amounts of time and effort.

I think it's interesting to go back to the formation of Amazon. The formation of Amazon is telling and sets the foundation for much of what it has become today. For those of us old enough to remember, Amazon started as an on-line book seller. Jeff Bezos determined that with the millions of book titles available, it would take significant square footage for any retail store to stock sufficient inventory and balance inventory. Rather, it would be much more efficient to carry a centralized inventory of books in a warehouse and set up an online store and search engine to ship books to consumers. It made sense and it worked but, much like the Amazon we see today, they perfected their search engine, the pricing and the entire shopping experience.

After all, roaming through a book store is like roaming a library trying to find a book that would interest you and if you had a specific title or book in mind, it might not be easy to find.

As I love to hear startup stories, one interesting tidbit when Amazon started was that book distributors required customers to order a minimum of ten books. Amazon couldn't afford to stock that many books, so they would order the one they wanted and then order nine copies of a book they knew was out of stock just to get going. Ingenuity at its best and even though Amazon started with books, all along Bezos knew he wanted to be a seller of all things. Being the biggest and best book seller wasn't good enough.

Amazon is an amazing company and has only been around for less than 25 years but has a market capitalization of $564 billion as of this writing and dominates in the e-commerce category. Market Capitalization is the value of a company traded on the stock market, calculated by multiplying the total number of shares by the current share price. A company that started as an on-line book seller has become a global marketplace offering products of all kinds, cloud services, logistics and much more. They are leading the charge in innovation and recently estimated to command over 40% market share for all online sales in the United States. Amazon is a juggernaut and dominating force, yet a company whose value doesn't reflect the traditional values determined by profit and EBITDA (Earnings Before Interest Taxes Depreciation and Amortization.)

In fact, public companies who compete with Amazon often cry foul as their shareholders demand profit and return on investment and claim Amazon doesn't have to play by the same rules they do. I am not a financial expert, but the value of Amazon is largely driven by their growth and market dominance and they are positioned for significant financial returns, but really that isn't their focus. Their focus is on serving the customer. Yes, that is what drives Amazon and if they serve the customer, the rest, or almost the rest will take care of itself.

While many think Amazon's success is because they sell so many things on-line, it goes much deeper than that. They, of any company, dominate because they have mastered the Hassle Quotient. They understand it better and use it more than anyone. They save their customers time, effort, are a price leader and have perfected the online experience.

Before we go there, I think it's important to understand the culture at Amazon. This is my perspective as an outsider and not ever working there. I have interviewed with Amazon and know they hire exceptionally smart and talented people and they all work at break neck speed.

Here are their leadership principles.

> 1. Customer Obsession. Leaders start with the customer and work backwards. They work vigorously to earn and keep customer trust. Although leaders pay attention to competitors, they obsess over customers.

Short and sweet but love how they use the word Obsession. It's not "Customers are First" or "We Love Customers", it is we are Obsessed with earning customer trust. Everything centers around the customer and it's pertinent that this is their first principle.

> 2. Ownership. Leaders are owners. They think long term and don't sacrifice long-term value for short-term results. They act on behalf of the entire company, beyond their own team. They never say, "that's not my job."

Exactly why Amazon, unlike so many other companies aren't concerned about this Quarter's financial results. How many companies have behaviors that are geared toward *this*

Quarter's results and we will worry about the next Quarter when it gets here. They produce sales and incentives all with the notion of hitting a top line sales number with little regard to the long-term impact.

> 3. Invent and Simplify. Leaders expect and require innovation and invention from their teams and always find ways to simplify. They are externally aware, look for new ideas from everywhere, and are not limited by "not invented here". As we do new things, we accept that we may be misunderstood for long period of time.

Amazon is as innovative as they come. Many companies are trying to play catch up to Amazon and when they think they are there, Amazon has leaped past them. I think Amazon Prime and two-day delivery are excellent examples of not only innovation, but simplicity. Amazon Prime members get free two-day shipping, a very simple message and millions support that. However, what's important to note is that this isn't their top principle. To Amazon, innovation and simplicity needs to be centered on the customer and not just innovation for innovation sake. Very important.

> 4. Are Right, A Lot. Leaders are right a lot. They have strong judgment and good instincts. They seek diverse perspectives and work to disconfirm their beliefs.

Wow oh wow. They work to disconfirm their beliefs. Most of us naturally work hard to confirm our beliefs and if you work hard enough will always confirm it. I like how Amazon takes the opposite approach. This also says a lot about the people Amazon hires, especially its leaders.

5. Learn and Be Curious. Leaders are never done learning and always seek to improve themselves. They are curious about new possibilities and act to explore them.

Wise words as we never should be done learning and improving. Important to state and practice that.

6. Hire and Develop the Best. Leaders raise the performance bar with every hire and promotion. They recognize exceptional talent, and willingly move them throughout the organization. Leaders develop leaders and take seriously their role in coaching others. We work on behalf of our people to invent mechanisms like Career Choice.

Being a leader is a tough job and not for everyone. I've often heard it said that the best sales person in an organization doesn't necessarily mean they will be the best sales leader. They may not have the proper skill sets to lead and mentor others and throughout my career, I've worked for some bad leaders and good leaders and ultimately decided that the person I reported to was as important as the company I worked for.

7. Insist on the Highest Standards. Leaders have relentlessly high standards – many people think these standards are unreasonably high. Leaders are continually raising the bar and driving their teams to deliver high quality products, services and processes. Leaders ensure that defects do not get sent down the line and that problems are fixed so they stay fixed.

I relate to this one as I used to say that if you are going to take the time to do anything, give it all you have. If you are going to mow the lawn, do the very best. Otherwise you risk having to do too much re-work. Wise thought by Amazon.

8. Think Big. Thinking small is a self-fulfilling prophecy. Leaders create and communicate a bold direction that inspires results. They think differently and look around corners for ways to serve customers.

If you don't think Amazon is constantly thinking big, you likely aren't reading the news. I love this quote from Steve Jobs that has similar thoughts.

"Here's to the crazy ones — the misfits, the rebels, the troublemakers, the round pegs in the square holes. The ones who see things differently — they're not fond of rules. You can quote them, disagree with them, glorify or vilify them, but the only thing you can't do is ignore them because they change things. They push the human race forward, and while some may see them as the crazy ones, we see genius, because the ones who are crazy enough to think that they can change the world, are the ones who do."

9. Bias for Action. Speed matters in business. Many decisions and actions are reversible and do not need extensive study. We value calculated risk taking.

I have heard a rumor that Amazon has a saying something to the effect of "Go cheetah on them." That could have a couple of meanings but if referring to a competitor, and the cheetah being the fastest animal on the planet, it could mean out run the competition and beat them.

10. Frugality. Accomplish more with less. Constraints breed resourcefulness, self-sufficiency and invention. There are no extra points for growing headcount, budget size or fixed expense.

Many entrepreneurs know that the last dollar is their dollar. Many venture capitalists will tell you that cash is king and that too much cash can ruin a company. I was probably wrong, but once in my career I coordinated a meeting of my direct reports and had them stay at a Red Roof Inn. It was the wrong thing to do, but I didn't admit it. I told the team that the KOA was sold out. I think they got the message that we all must be careful with our funds and budgets are critical. Didn't do that again but didn't host any meetings in 5-star resorts either.

11. Earn Trust. Leaders listen attentively, speak candidly, and treat others respectfully. They are vocally self-critical, even when doing so is awkward or embarrassing. Leaders do not believe their or their team's body odor smells of perfume. They benchmark themselves and their teams against the best.

Nothing better than humility in a leader but it is essential to listen and react if you are going to be a good leader.

---

12. Dive Deep. Leaders operate at all levels, stay connected to the details, audit frequently, and are skeptical when metrics and anecdote differ. No task is beneath them.

While I am not a huge fan of the television show Undercover Boss, I find it amusing how much the boss learns by taking the role of one of the lower level workers. Great leaders understand the details of their business down to the rudimentary level.

---

13. Have Backbone; Disagree and Commit. Leaders are obligated to respectfully challenge decisions when they disagree, even when doing so is uncomfortable or exhausting. Leaders have conviction and are tenacious. They do not compromise for the sake of social cohesion. Once a decision is determined, they commit wholly.

Agree. Great leaders make commitments and follow through.

> 14. Deliver Results. Leaders focus on the key inputs for their business and deliver them with the right quality and in a timely fashion. Despite setbacks, they rise to the occasion and never settle.

One of my favorite sayings is; "Don't confuse activity with results."

Amazon isn't restricted to selling items. They have a logistics company, Fulfillment by Amazon, a powerful web hosting service called Amazon Web Services and a competitive offering to Netflix. I don't know all the services they have, but they are a power house and a dominant company any way one wants to look at them. They are the 4th most valuable company in the world, only behind Apple, Alphabet (the parent company of Google) and Microsoft and are the 8th largest employer in the U.S. with 180,000 employees and 300,000 worldwide. The formula works!

By understanding their leadership principles, I believe it gives great insight into what makes Amazon tick. This isn't a book about Amazon, it's about what formula is used by the most dominating companies in today's (2018) market. Many people suggest that Amazon is the beast it is today because it is an online e-commerce site that offers many products. And those people would be correct, but that is only part of the story. After all, Amazon has experimented with actual retail stores and in 2017 purchased Whole Foods which has brick and mortar in its DNA.

If you take the *Hassle Quotient* and break it down, in its most basic form, Amazon has used this formula to spur its growth and now dominate. At its core, Amazon is a marketplace offering customers a wide variety of merchandise from which to select. Some of that merchandise doesn't sit in Amazon warehouses but fulfilled by companies who simply understand the market presence of Amazon, its traffic and uses it to sell their items.

Amazon, I believe, gives consumers more options than any other e-commerce site. If you are looking for anything, you will see hundreds, if not thousands of options. They allow you to shop and compare. They don't just offer one brand, or one model but understand that the average consumer wants choices. I would suggest that Amazon has a powerful search engine as they manage millions of SKUs and it is very easy to insert a variety of keywords or phrases to find what you are seeking. Then, they allow the user to sort the options in a variety of ways, but their default is "let me show you the most popular" in order as you might be like millions of others and we at Amazon want to save you time. There it is. They want to save me time in my search. Brilliant and one of the key components to the *Hassle Quotient*.

Another very cool feature they offer is customer reviews. And, there aren't just a few, there are thousands of reviews and they aren't biased in that they only show the best. They openly show the good and the bad. Even better, since a consumer cannot touch and feel the product, they allow for consumers to ask questions. It's highly likely that a question you might have about a product has been asked already and it is recorded to be seen.

Now imagine you are at a store, say Walmart, and you want to know about a product you are considering. Would you walk up and down the aisles and say, "Excuse me, but I'm thinking of buying this toothbrush and wondering if you have any experience with this brand?" Of course, you wouldn't. And what if you wanted to know about the durability of that tooth brush? First, you must find someone who has bought it and then get their opinion. In the matter of seconds, I can do that on the Amazon marketplace.

For me, it's not unusual to go to Amazon first and read reviews even if I end up buying the product from a different company. Granted, Amazon has, in the past, used reviews from paid parties but have eliminated that practice as they understand that we consumers want the real skinny on something and not from someone who was provided the product in exchange for their opinion or who was paid to provide their opinion. We want recommendations from our neighbors, the people we trust. Amazon also has a cool feature where consumers can ask questions that previous buyers answer. Most of the time, I find that the question I was thinking has been answered. That really is helpful for me.

In the Amazon marketplace, products available with Prime are clearly marked and highlighted. In the Amazon marketplace, you can add items to wish lists, quickly order repeat items from past orders and have the Amazon Dash button. The dash button allows you to automatically replenish whatever supplies you use frequently. Let's say you order laundry detergent once a month, or dog food every two weeks. With the Amazon Dash button, they make it easier to place those orders. Again, take the time and effort away and consumers will increase allegiance for whatever is being sold.

One thing I want to make very clear, is that Amazon understands all the components of the *Hassle Quotient*. They make their online experience, easy, fast, simple and with the marketplace impact, one can compare multiple items to get the best price. No driving to retail stores to see if they have the product you want, can deliver in one or two days, even same-day in some markets, and have a return policy and process that is extremely simple and easy. In fact, I bought a $7 item once that I ultimately didn't want and when I went to return it was told to just keep it. They recognized that the cost of returning and processing was more than the cost of me keeping it. However, Amazon masters data collection and analysis, and I'm confident that if I had a habit of doing this, I would be stopped.

Amazon has mastered the art of navigating websites. They know the value of minimizing the number of clicks a consumer must make, the number of pages one needs to go through and every step in between. With Amazon, I have an option of buying anything with a single click. Yes, single click and I don't have to go through the checkout process! Amazing savings of time and effort. I get the value I seek with the product I want and the experience, especially compared to other sites and getting in my car to go to the mall, it's just perfect for me.

Amazon has mastered all facets of the *Hassle Quotient*. They save consumers time. They require little effort by giving access 24x7x365, have compelling price points with their marketplace approach with multiple options and the experience is great.

In logistics, many speak of the Amazon Effect. That is, free shipping and delivery within 2 days. Amazon has created a brand-new user experience that reduces the time it takes to get product to anyone and lowered the cost with free shipping. That has placed tremendous strain on conventional retailers and even other e-commerce companies to provide at least the same experience.

As you might suspect, not everyone wants to cooperate with Amazon. As a marketplace Amazon will market and fulfill your products but many believe that Amazon could use the data they collect about your services and products as a weapon against you. Amazon has enough money and clout to put nearly any product out of business, if not the whole company. Supposedly, there is an internal expression within Amazon that is something to the tune of "Go Cheetah on Them." I take that to mean either out-run the competition or out run and take them down. If anyone can do that, it's Amazon.

I know of a collaboration where multiple retailers, being threatened by the "Amazon Effect" are putting together a distribution network to enable two-day shipping nationwide and offer essentially the same level of service Amazon has pioneered. There are companies that do not want Amazon to control their customer or distribution channel. Simply by owning data, that can be a threat to some companies. They don't want Amazon to know their customers, their price points, their product mix, what selling best, what is selling the least and how customers feel about their products. I don't know if that will be successful, but such collaboration is evidence that many retailers feel the Amazon threat.

It's a real lesson for others. If you or your company have a have a website, and you should, you need to learn lessons from Amazon. I cannot stress this enough. People want to know within seconds what it is you do when they land on your site. That's right. You have seconds to hit them with your elevator pitch and it best not be confusing, or they will be gone. They will move on to another site.

Each key stroke is important, and you need to set up your navigation to ensure your customers and prospects spend as little time and effort navigating your web-site. Engineer it to be modern, easy to navigate and efficient for your customers!

Amazon has incredible sales at approximately $178 billion annually. However, that number will likely be quite outdated by the time people read that. In their latest year, they realized a profit of around $3 billion, not what might be expected from a traditional company, but Amazon is anything but traditional. And they think in an unconventional way.

They have a market share of 43% and spend over $5 billion in shipping costs, most of which is absorbed by the company and not passed on to customers. They have a remarkable 43% market share and growing even though they have thousands of e-commerce competitors. The competitors don't offer the extensive product line that Amazon does, but thousands of companies sell products online.

Loyalty Program

In 2005, Amazon pioneered a loyalty program that resulted in phenomenal growth. The created Amazon Prime, a program that offered free, two-day shipping on many of the items they stocked. It costs a customer $119 annually (recently increased from $99) to become a Prime member but in addition to free shipping, they get many other benefits, such as access to Amazon videos and a wider variety of music. Even though Prime membership was increased in 2018 to $119 per year, it is still a great value as the break-even for any consumer is less than 12 orders per year assuming an average order costs a conservative $10 to ship. In addition to "free" shipping, Prime members are promised

2-day shipping. When Amazon launched Prime they set the bar for nearly everyone involved in e-commerce to offer "free" shipping along with faster two-day shipping regardless of consumer location. With transportation companies facing increasing costs due to driver shortages, higher fuel, insurance and equipment costs, it's placed great pressure on anyone trying to compete with Amazon's Prime service.

Even with 100 million Prime members, or over half of all households, Amazon must subsidize shipping for this class of membership. However, Amazon recognizes the lifetime value of a customer and has determined it worthy of the shipping subsidy as they spend more than $119 in shipping cost for the average Amazon customer. Amazon Prime is a great example of taking the hassle out of shopping and the cost out of shipping. I cannot think of a loyalty program as impactful and one that has garnered Amazon such amazing market share.

Prime has become one of the best, if not the best, loyalty program on the planet. My wife is a Prime member and I tag along on her account as do my married kids. During the checkout process, one can quickly and easily switch payment methods and shipping addresses and so with a single membership, my wife's Prime account supports 4 families. Yes, she must share her password credentials and worry about someone gaining access, but she's alerted on every purchase electronically so can monitor who is using her Prime account. I nearly made a mistake when I bought her a birthday present signed in as her. At the last minute, I changed to my regular account, so she wouldn't be notified of her new Fitbit and ruin the surprise. Yes, it was painful paying for shipping as I wasn't accustomed to that. One would think Amazon would find ways to prevent the sharing of a Prime account, but I believe they are more driven by sales and customer obsession than finding those who take advantage of the system. It works.

As previously stated, Amazon is subsidizing shipping costs to the tune of between $5-7 billion per year. The $119 annual fee, which was recently increased, does not cover the actual cost of shipping. That's right, they are spending **billions** to support the Prime program. But it works. A conventionally thinking company might not consider offering totally free shipping. After all, how much better would Amazon be performing from a financial perspective if they simply broke even on shipping? Imagine the happy shareholders by adding up to $7 billion per year onto profits. Most companies would do that, but Amazon isn't most companies and they fully understand the long-term impact, the life cycle value of a Prime customer and how subsidizing shipping with Prime members makes them a dominant company.

Innovation

Amazon has a history of innovation, not only for the services and products they sell to consumers and companies, but internal innovation to help improve customer experience and lower costs. Amazon has pioneered a couple of well-known products that epitomize the *Hassle Quotient*. While there were some e-readers on the market, when Amazon introduced and refined their Kindle over time, it became the mainstay for electronic books. What better way to reduce the amount of time to get a book then have it downloaded instantaneously? How about a book that opens where you were last reading? How about a device that is backlit, so you can read in the dark? What size font do you want? Saves time, effort and a better user experience. Sound familiar?

Remember how I said people are lazy, or prefer to exert less effort if given a choice? Anyone familiar with the Amazon Echo understands what I mean about exerting effort. Rather than pull out my connected smart device, I now can simply speak to the Echo and it will get me my answers. After all, typing can be physically draining, right? Or, with a smart device, I must open my music app and find a song I want to play. With the Echo, I simply tell Alexa to play that song. Wow! So, Amazon has incorporated elements of the Hassle Quotient into their products they invented.

Amazon innovated a device called the Dash button which is designed to more easily re-order commonly used, often lower-priced items that are used in households. With the single click of a button one can re-order items such as laundry detergent, dog food or diapers. Could Amazon require less effort and save more time than providing a button that re-orders product for you? I don't know of anyone else offering this level of convenience that, by the way, turns into incredible sales revenue.

And just when you think you might have Amazon figured out, they put something new on the board and make it reality. Just when retailers are closing brick and mortar stores by the hundreds, Amazon decided to create a few brick and mortar stores but, of course, with a twist.

After testing a concept with its own employees for a year, Amazon is opening a store to the public that allows anyone to browse, grab and walk out with your merchandise without having to endure the checkout line. No, it's not free merchandise, they have devised technology to know what you have chosen and taken.

It's a convenience store (really convenient with no checkout lines) with proprietary technology comprised of hundreds of cameras and sensors that only require a new Amazon app to shop at the store. Amazon knows that the bane of every shopper is the wasted time and frustration of a checkout line. They aim to fundamentally change how grocery shopping is done and make the user experience better.

Obviously, this technology is very complex and sophisticated and likely before broad rollout will go through more immense testing but, as a consumer, I like the thought of it. I think it is the forefront to massive changes and much like the robotics used in Amazon distribution centers, will speed the customer's experience, but also reduce costs. When Amazon reduces costs, they profit by reducing prices and gaining more customers. Again, an example of how they think differently. They could put all the savings to the bottom line, but that isn't their end game.

In the 100 years since the first modern supermarket, no one has ever solved the problem of long lines and wait time for checkout. Many stores simply add lanes that are often not staffed. According to Amazon, seventy-three percent of consumers they surveyed say one of the things they most want from a company is that they value their time. Get it? Time is our most precious commodity. Amazon understands that, and they asked consumers and now working even more diligently on a time-saving brick and mortar solution.

Here's how the new concept works. The store is about the size of an average convenience store. Customers must first download the Amazon Go app and link it to a payment method. Then they open the app on their smart device (phone or tablet) and scan it at one of the turnstiles to enter the store.

Once inside, cameras in the ceiling, sensors on the shelves and a massive amount of computing power track every item the consumer picks up and what goes into their bags or pockets. As they move through the store, each item is added to the digital tab in the app. If they pick something up but then put it back, the system knows it and removes it from the virtual shopping basket in the app.

The technology is named Just Walk Out because that's all a shopper must do when they are done. Amazon admits there are challenges to opening these stores on a broad-scale basis. And there are challenges to broadening the application to the equivalent of multi-department grocery stores. Items that are charged on a per pound basis are a challenge as are fresh meats and deli items. The point is Amazon is taking bold steps to change the biggest pain a consumer faces when shopping and translating that into a better experience at lower costs.

The other important factor to understand is the amount of real-time data Amazon can collect on consumer buying behaviors. They can gather customer data about likes, dislikes and even what people pick up and then put back, all of which can be analyzed and turned into future stocking decisions.

Logistics

At its core, Amazon, in my opinion, is a logistics company. Logistics is about having the right product at the right time and at the right cost. I mean who doesn't want "free shipping"? Who wouldn't want their order to be delivered within two days? Heck give me same-day if it doesn't cost me more!

Customers are increasing their demands and what was once satisfactory delivery quickly becomes obsolete when someone like Amazon changes the rules and changes performance. When Amazon first got started, they, like most others, had to use conventional shipping means such as the Post Office, UPS, FedEx, LTL and truckload. Now, they have leased aircraft and set up their own air network, have purchased thousands of over-the-road trailers, created options for small last mile companies to deliver packages, even using employees to deliver packages on their way home.

Amazon has planned or operations over 140 distribution centers in the United State to fulfill their promise of two-day delivery to any point in the country. If you think about the number of products they stock, the amount of inbound merchandise they order, it really blows my mind. They use the latest technology for everything and have robots operating in many of their DCs to speed order processing and minimize costs. It's an incredible investment they have made and a significant barrier to any competitor equaling or beating them at what they do.

As stated, they started shipping with conventional for-hire transportation service providers like UPS, FedEx, USPS, LTL carriers and truckload carriers. However, over time, as volumes have increased, they have developed new methods of shipping to cut its cost and better control service performance, or the customer experience. In 2013, United

Parcel Service, then one of Amazon's primary small package carriers fundamentally under-estimated the volume of packages they would need to handle during the peak Christmas season. Service delays were numerous and even some consumers didn't receive packages until after Christmas Day and many of those were Amazon packages.

It was at that juncture that Amazon decided not to let an outside force have such dramatic influence over their customer shipping experience. The put, and continue to put in place, multiple tactics to deliver to their promise and to try and reduce the deficit they run between shipping charges paid by consumers and those they absorb.

One program developed is called Flex. That is where full or part-time contractors, using their own vehicles can deliver Amazon packages in their communities. They also have experimented with warehouse employees, again using their own vehicles, delivering packages to consumers on their way home. They have experimented with delivering packages to the trunks of cars while consumers are working. They have also implemented a publicized unattended home delivery, where a delivery person can access the front door of one's residence and set packages inside. In addition to a lock that could be exclusively accessed by a driver, there is a camera inside the house to record the delivery. I believe that service was mostly in response to a growing problem of packages being stolen from front porches. Not sure the status of that experiment as multiple problems uncovered. That doesn't stop Amazon from innovating.

For more remote small packages, Amazon hires contracted carriers to pick up at their distribution centers in the wee hours of the morning and then deliver to every neighborhood post office (called DDU) in time for same-day package delivery. It's very cost-effective delivering to the last handling point for the USPS and no one blankets coverage like the Post Office.

Most recently, Amazon announced they are creating business opportunities for entrepreneurs who want to start their delivery companies. For as little as $10,000, a person can start their own business delivering Amazon packages. Supposedly, one can lease Amazon branded delivery vehicles, obtain insurance, accounting and payroll services and even obtain discounted gas cards. They are changing the game very quickly.

There has been speculation that Amazon might compete with FedEx and UPS and open their shipping to anyone. Personally, I'm skeptical of that. Without doubt, Amazon has interest in controlling the service performance and lowering the cost for both outbound and inbound shipping. That will keep them busy a long time and they have the volume and shipment density to effectively do that. I think developing a for-hire network could get in the way of accomplishing their core mission.

They are going to control the delivery costs and service and not be dependent upon third party companies to control their customer experience. They are big enough to do that.

Someone could, and probably will someday write a comprehensive book solely on Amazon. They have and continue to innovate in so many areas. Here is an Amazon innovation that blows my mind. After over four years in waiting, Amazon was issued a patent in January 2018 for use of a mobile 3D printer. For simplicity purposes, they want exclusivity to having 3D printers in trucks that can be printing parts or products as the truck is on its way to the customer. The ability to dynamically create things and especially parts, on the fly, and deliver within an hour or hours is customer-service at its best. I don't want to dwell on 3D printing, but it is becoming more mainstream and is especially agile for creating parts. And it doesn't have to be cheap plastic parts. Currently, 3D printers are creating titanium aircraft parts. That is how sophisticated it is getting.

Let's say, you had an HVAC technician working on you're A/C on a 100-degree day and needed a critical part. Maybe the technician doesn't stock it in his truck, or maybe not even back at the shop. No problem, I'll have Amazon deliver it within the hour as they can print it. All we must do is send the file for the specs. That is where this is going. It saves the consumer time, probably money and provides an experience no one is accustomed to.

The scariest part of Amazon is they are not resting on their laurels. They are investing in new processes, new technologies and getting into new lines of business. Companies need to pay heed. You can never rest. Never assume you have reduced the amount of time it takes for a customer to engage you. Never assume you have minimized the effort it takes for a customer to purchase from you. For certain, you can never assume that you have taken cost out of your offering, so you can provide more competitive products or services, and you can always improve the user experience of your customer. Just keep asking them, they'll tell you.

If I were to assess Amazon and determine its *Hassle Quotient* from my perspective, it would be as low as any company I have engaged.

Chapter 5 – Uber and Others

Uber & Lyft

One of my favorite companies that has transformed an industry is Uber. While I don't believe that Uber is any better than someone like Lyft, they got first-mover advantage and have significantly greater market share than its competitors simply because they have more capacity or drivers, and thus, can save customers time by having more drivers available and located closer to riders than their competitors.

It does bring up another point however. Uber, Lyft and others have transformed an industry. It's not just that they have duplicated the old model and try to do it better, or out-market current providers, they dominate. I would imagine that somewhere in an original business plan, Uber spoke of disrupting the taxi or cab business. So many startups use the term "disrupt" and I admit I have been guilty of using that term. However, I really prefer the word transform than disrupt. I think of disruption when a fullback plows through a defensive front at the goal line. That is disruption. It can cause pain and significant movement. Whereas, transformation is about change and typically in a positive manner.

Either way, Uber has absolutely transformed the movement of people business that was once dominated by the taxi and limousine business. Here is a company that lost nearly $1.5

billion in the 3rd Quarter of 2017 and yet has a market capitalization or value of nearly $50 billion. Yes, that is a loss with a "b" and in a single quarter. Granted, they reached a market cap of nearly $70 billion and then had multiple internal issues including their founder stepping down as CEO, but 99% of all start-ups that lose that much money would be out of business after releasing results like that. So, what gives?

Uber and Lyft both have transformed the industry but most importantly, whether they know it or not, have adopted and use the Hassle Quotient as their strategy. The business model is brilliant as they have embraced the "Shared economy" theory where they leverage existing assets, cars that people own, and provide a source of income for anyone with a car that can leverage an under-utilized asset. Uber provides a business opportunity for any individual with a relatively new car and quickly set them up to start earning additional income while providing a much-needed service to those needing rides. It is much less capital-intensive capital model than the cab company model. Granted, Uber perhaps has skipped some critical steps such as complete vetting and qualifying of drivers and not paying heed to the various state and city permits required of a taxi operation. They are also known for bullying their way into markets only to leave if threatened with the same burdens placed on the cab industry.

Much like Amazon, the taxi industry is constantly crying foul on Uber and Lyft as they claim they don't have to go through the same certification processes that the cab industry does. While that may be true, the real reason the taxi industry is hurting, is that Uber and Lyft provide what consumers want. They provide a service that requires less time and effort to engage, costs less than a cab service and a much better overall experience. The taxi industry has also failed to understand that there is a lot more to the Uber and Lyft formula for success than simply adding a mobile app to their repertoire. You may have noticed that many cab companies have added an app, but, besides that, not much else has changed.

Let me give you my experience with using a taxi/cab service. First, unless you are needing a ride from an airport or a hotel, you cannot easily locate a cab. New York city might be an exception. In the old days you would have to find a phone book to get a number for a cab company, but now you can use your smart phone and get a phone number. You call the company and talk to a dispatcher who asks your address and then tells you that a cab is on the way and will be there in 15-20 minutes. That is their standard pitch, as they have no idea and won't dispatch the driver until you hang up.

A lot of time and effort to engage them. Now, if you are at an airport or hotel, it's simply a matter of finding the loading point and waiting in line. However, whether you call or get in line, the rest of the experience is the same for all.

Once you get in the cab, tell the driver the address of your destination. You might have to yell that given that there is likely a thick plexiglass divider between the back seat and front. It is like a simulated police car experience, though I have not had the pleasure of being in the back seat of a police car. After you have communicated your destination, you are likely to be asked if you have cash. I assume the driver wants cash, so they don't have to report the full fare to the IRS, or maybe it's just to avoid the 3% credit card fee. Regardless, most of the time the rider is going to be asked, which is really a nuisance.

I always use the excuse that it's company policy to pay for fares using my credit card just because I don't want to use cash. Once that is settled, the driver takes off and it isn't long before you notice the springs in the seat are trying to get intimate with your back side. But, you are only slightly distracted with that as the driving habits of the driver are getting your attention as they often use very liberal driving rules.

I find that I don't enjoy conversing with cab drivers as many have a dialect that I have a hard time understanding. I'm not biased as these truly are hard-working people and must wait hours sometimes to catch their next fare. But I prefer to stay to myself. Once at my destination, I need to hand over my credit card, either through a hole in the plexiglass or get out and through the front window. They then fumble with a credit card processing device attached to their smart phone or have a full-blown card processing machine. Once they run that, often with problems, they hand you the receipt and you can insert a tip, total the amount and exist the vehicle. All done.

Now, let's compare that to Uber or Lyft. Wherever I am, hotel or airport or other, I open my smart phone app and request a ride while providing my destination. I am quickly alerted that a driver has accepted my request and informed how many minutes away or time before I will be picked up. I have access to the driver's vehicle, his or her mug shot, the license plate and feedback rating from other riders. I can track my car as it progresses to me and when it arrives, I hop in and away we go.

One of the best parts of the Uber or Lyft experience is I know the price up front. When I type in my destination (it already knows my origin), I receive a solid estimate of the price for the trip. Yes, it can deviate if the driver takes a different route to avoid traffic or we get stuck in traffic for an inordinate amount of time, but it's typically very close. Whereas, with a cab, they might have some complicated formula on the side of their door, I really don't have a clue what the fare is going to be until the trip is completed.

I do get the pleasure of watching that annoying meter however. I believe cab companies start with a base amount, typically something like $2.50, though there might be a surcharge if it's originating from an airport property. After all, we must compensate the driver for their wait time, or maybe there is a little *"something-something"* for the airport authority or city in the extra fee. I suspect the latter. But I digress. Typically, there is a base fee, and then a mileage charge for every quarter-mile, but then they add something for standing still at like a stop light. Boy do I hate those stop lights when the ticker just keeps on churning.

I'm the kind of guy who likes to know up front the financial commitment I am about to make. I'm okay with formulas and how the rate is going to be determined, but with cabs, there is always a variable or two I don't know, like time and distance. I like to know what I am going to spend before I spend it. With cabs, you have no clue in most cases. Yes, there are some exceptions but as a rule, it's a blank check and that leaves most, including me, with a bad taste in my mouth.

With Uber, the car I am riding in is much like my car. It has no plexiglass and the seats are as comfortable as my personal car. The driver is courteous, often offering me a bottle of water and I can choose to engage in conversation or not. Maybe that is because the driver knows they are going to be evaluated and the results available for future riders. I don't have to tell the driver where I am going, they already know. I am assured they are going to take the most expedient route as they have an incentive to provide as many rides in a day as they can. Once we arrive at our destination, I simply say, "thank you" and exit the vehicle. We are done. I get an electronic receipt, the offer to rate the driver and a request to tip the driver if I feel so inclined.

Bottom line is it took me less time and effort to engage, cost me less than a cab and the experience was significantly better all the way around. If Uber or Lyft were to charge more than a taxi, I for one, would likely do that, but that would only make them a very good or great company and not a dominant one.

The other thing is I don't trust cab drivers. Recently, I traveled to Orlando for a trade show and I was responsible for setting up our booth. I admit I took a little later flight than I should have and when I landed knew it was going to be tight to assemble the booth in the time window specified by the trade association. Orlando, at that time, had some rule that didn't allow for Uber to provide service from the airport. You could take Uber to the airport, but not from it. So, I assume someone was getting paid off somewhere, but I digress yet again. I didn't have time to take a hotel shuttle to get off the airport property and then take Uber.

So, I opted for a cab and went through the typical experience and gave the driver my destination hotel name and address. I am not from Orlando. While I have been there numerous times, I must trust the cabbie that they are going to take me there in the most direct route. I am not anal enough to pull up GPS and track the route and question the driver. I should have. To make a long story, short, I arrived at the hotel about 30 minutes later and the meter read $50. I gave him my credit card, tipped him $5 (yes, a minimum tip, I know) and was done.

When the conference concluded, I had ample time to hail an Uber and did that. Without saying anything, the driver knew I was going to the airport. However, given my trip to the hotel, I decided to measure, and 14 minutes and $16 later, I exited the Uber vehicle and later tipped the driver via the mobile app. Yes, my cabbie took advantage of me for at least $25. I imagine he waited in line at the airport for an hour or so and was going to maximize his fare at my expense. I guess I can't really blame him, but it is an indication of a broken system and one that falls downhill to the consumer, me. Unfortunately for the cab industry, I hold a grudge and it is going to take very special circumstances for me to hail a cab again.

I would be remiss if I didn't note that Uber can charge less than a cab company because they don't play by the same rules and don't have all the expenses that a taxi company pays. Uber is a broker when you peel back the onion. They provide the marketing and infrastructure to offer a better service than a cab company would and use independent contractors who own vehicles to deliver the service. I make it a habit of asking every Uber or Lyft driver how long they have been doing Uber or Lyft and it is rare that anyone ever answers more than a year. Many of their drivers are between jobs or doing Uber or Lyft to supplement their income. Maybe they are buying a house or planning on getting married or taking a big vacation. They all love that they can set their own hours and work as much or as little as they want. They are operating their own business and are truly independent.

However, because Uber sets the fare, and pays the driver a percentage of the fare, all too often the fares aren't enough to cover the full operating expense of a vehicle. I have seen Uber advertisements to draw interest stating one can make $17 per hour. A driver can make that amount, but you must take out operating expenses such as gas, maintenance, wear and tear and depreciation. When you do that, I think the residual is minimum wage or even less. I have a son-in-law who did Uber for a while and quickly learned to only do it when it was peak pricing, but that is hard to sustain. I do understand that Uber, with the new management team in place has instituted the allowance of tips and I believe have raised fares somewhat to help. However, at the end of the day, it's all about supply and demand. If there are drivers willing to do it, and there are, Uber will maintain its current practices.

Bottom line is Uber and Lyft have transformed the industry and taken the cab industry from an experience that takes time and effort to engage, costs a lot with a crummy experience, to one that is easy, simple, fast to engage, at a lower cost and much better experience and now dominate this space.

Recently, an autonomous (driverless) car struck and killed a pedestrian in Arizona which is absolutely tragic. Maybe, Uber is going too fast in taking the next step with cost reduction before the technology is ready. I think it's obvious that Uber has a vision of "car bots" that are rapidly available and operate at a lower cost than a human behind the wheel. However, safety in the passenger transportation business is paramount to everything else.

Netflix

One of the very best illustrations of a company using the *Hassle Quotient* formula is the story of Netflix. Now, I hate to admit that I'm old enough to have experienced television as a kid with 3 channels, (NBC, CBS and ABC) and if we got lucky, maybe a channel from UHF by crimpling some aluminum foil on the antenna and twirling it around a bit. That might be a foreign concept to a few of you. The next big advancement was the remote-control TV. Back then, it was nothing like it is today. Our first remote was about as large as your hand and when you pressed the forward or backward channel button, it would make this loud racket as each channel changed. Can you imagine a remote today making noise? But it was amazing technology and so much easier than getting out of your chair and flipping the channel with your hand.

From there, of course, cable TV came about and opened our world to a wide variety of channels and the remote was a must to surf TV and find something to watch. A real break-through was when the VHS which was invented in 1977. Now, you could obtain videos, especially movies, that you could insert into a VHS player and watch at your convenience. If you were trying to watch a movie on TV, especially in the cable era with so many channels, you might pop in after it had started, or halfway through. With this new toy, it didn't take long for stores to pop up that would rent you movies. How convenient! However, it was important to rewind the tapes before turning them back to the store or face a fine.

The VHS cycle lasted a good while if comparing to technology cycles of today. It lasted a good 18 years until the Digital Video Recorder, or DVD format, was created in 1995. Say goodbye to those pesky rewind fees. However, to take advantage of the higher resolution, smaller medium and many more capabilities, we had to buy DVD players. It was well worth it.

I think the company that dominated the VHS and DVD rental space most recognizable to everyone, was Blockbuster. I believe at one time, there was a Blockbuster as close to you as your local post office. At least, they needed to be somewhat close to make it convenient for the consumer to rent from them. Blockbuster started in 1985 and was acquired by an investment team led by Wayne Huizenga in 1987. At its height, Blockbuster had 9,000 stores in 2004. Oh, how the mighty can fall.

A short six years later in 2010, Blockbuster declared bankruptcy for the purpose or re-organizing, but the re-organization ultimately failed and closed its final stores in 2013. Even by today's standard of losing retailers left and right, that was a meteoric fall.

What happened? Netflix happened, that's what. Here is a telling statistic. In the year 2000, Blockbuster collected a whopping $800 million in late fees. That was 16% of their total revenue. How do you feel about late fees? That's right. If you are like me, you understand them, but hate to pay them, no matter how little they are.

I remember many Friday and Saturday nights going over to our local Blockbuster and immediately heading for the "New Releases" section. Couldn't wait to see what had come out that week. All too often, and most of the time, the new release section looked like an underpriced buffet. Anything good was gone and only marginal new releases might be available. Then I would meander through the other 80% of the store looking at older movies to see if there was anything that looked interesting, that I hadn't seen.

If memory serves me, Blockbuster charged $1 per day late fee. So, with $800 million in one year, that adds up to a lot of late movies. One of those who experienced this late fee was a gentleman by the name of Reed Hastings. He rented Apollo 13 and was late to the tune of $40! That didn't sit well with Mr. Hastings and 2 years later, on the premise of the *Hassle Quotient*, founded a company named Netflix. Heard of them?

When Netflix started, their goal was to make it simpler and easier to shop and receive DVDs as well as make it much more convenient to return DVDs. Their only disadvantage was that you couldn't decide to run down to Netflix last minute on a Friday evening and rent your favorite movie. You did that online and it was mailed to you, typically receiving it next day. You see, Mr. Hastings, like Jeff Bezos, understood that the number and titles of DVDs was immense, and they could be much more efficient storing them in regional warehouses than they could in many retail shops. The inventory rationalization would allow for greater efficiency and for certain, they would make the return process much simpler.

When they mailed the DVD in their famous red envelope, they included a postage-paid return envelope and you only had to drop it in your mailbox and not have to leave the comfort of your own home to avoid late fees. Netflix also came up with an unlimited plan whereby a consumer could pay a monthly fee for unlimited number of DVDs per month. That was a far better value than the $2.99 per day for a new release or $4.99 for 3-day rental.

Let's stop and review. To become a dominant company, you must meet all elements of the *Hassle Quotient.* You need to save your customer time and effort. Netflix passed with shining colors on the effort part. You could shop from the comfort of your home on your PC or smart device and more quickly find the movie or show of your choice. No hassle with getting in the car, driving to the local store to maybe, or maybe not, find your movie in stock, or find one you liked. However, time spent was questionable. The soonest you could get a movie from Netflix was next day, so if it was a last-minute urge to watch a DVD, you would be out of luck with Netflix. Third, if you were an infrequent DVD watcher, you might be better off economically "paying by the drink" with Blockbuster. If you tended to watch several DVDs per month, it was cheaper to subscribe to the Netflix plan.

Hands down, the customer experience with Netflix was superior. Rarely was Netflix out of stock whereas, Blockbuster was constantly out of stock on new releases. Secondly, the return process, while easy, forced me into another trip, or simply remembering I needed to return the rented DVD today to avoid late charges. And the online search experience is far superior than trudging up and down aisles to pick up empty DVD packets and read descriptions if I could find anything in the genre I wanted in the first place.

For those of you keeping score, time saved was almost, but the amount of effort was clearly superior, the cost lower and the overall user experience far superior to the option of renting a movie from a store.

In 2007, the one component of the formula that wasn't better was solved when Netflix introduced streaming. Who knew that streaming would be possible when the internet was invented, or those remarkable DVDs were created? Streaming! Now, had Netflix not adopted and led the video streaming parade, I might be writing of them like Blockbuster, that is, in past tense. Had another company come along and said; "I know, we are going to take the hardware out of the media equation and enable streaming of content and completely rid consumer of dealing with inbound and outbound mail, and late fees, etc.", that alone would have been reason for a company to compete.

It didn't happen that way of course. Netflix transformed itself and allowed for streaming and now met all the elements of the *Hassle Quotient* by enabling instantaneous content delivery, no effort, low cost and a superior overall customer experience. Around 110 million subscribers later, with a market cap of $95 billion and producing its own content, the future is bright for Netflix.

Yes, Netflix has competitors. One of the more notable is Amazon. However, they are competing on price as it is a part of their Prime membership. They haven't done anything to lower the amount of time and effort to engage them nor make the customer experience better. I'm sure they have millions of members using their video service, but they weren't the first mover here, Netflix was and a perfect example of a company who used the *Hassle Quotient* to dominate. I'm sure if I asked Mr. Hastings if he used the *Hassle Quotient* to found Netflix, he would look at me like I was a nut. He would say heck no. He would say I wanted to create a company that offered a better experience, at a lower price that required less time and effort by the customer. That is what he likely would say and that is exactly what he did.

Google/Alphabet

When I first heard the name internet and world wide web, and had it explained, I kind of understood it, but really didn't understand the scale and scope it would become. What started as a research product became Google in 1996. They understood that the content of the internet was and would become so massive there needed to be a way to search the content.

It has become a verb. I will "Google" that to find out. Yes, there are competitor search engines, but Google dominates. From the beginning Google operated an interesting business model. What might have been a subscription service for the consumer became an easy-to-use tool that is part of my everyday life for sure. Had they started with a subscription service, it wouldn't have become the dominant company it is. Providing a valuable time-saving service to the consumer, making it easy and free to use has been its mainstay. They have added offerings such as Google documents, Google email (Gmail), Maps and a lot more. However, their mainstay is their remarkable and robust search engine.

They reverse-engineered the company by deploying the *Hassle Quotient* for us the consumer, making their engine simple, easy, little effort, no cost and a great experience and then parlayed the power of data aggregation and then sell that to people and companies that care. And those people and companies care to the tune of about $90 billion per year.

Companies spend an inordinate amount of money setting up their website to be "searched" by Google. Using complex algorithms, Google's goal is to point consumers to the most relevant data and information they can so that consumers continue to use Google and they stay number one in the search engine race. Companies want to be found and spend a lot of money on ads via Google and even with marketing gurus to set up their websites with the right content and relevancy to be found. It's a big deal to end up on page 1 of any Google search and best if you are number one. In fact, if you ever do a search for a product, you might see some ads for that product in other areas of the internet. Yes, they are very smart about understanding each and every consumer and aggregating that to market and sell to those who are looking to offer products and services via the web.

There have been multiple iterations within Google's search engine between Ad Words that used to be listed on the right of the results page to now just Ad pages that are clearly marked.

I graduated with a degree in Marketing in the late 1970's and it absolutely isn't relevant today. Marketing, in today's world is all about website relevance, search engine optimization and digital marketing. I think marketing is far more a science today than when I was in school. If I were to do it again, I would *minor in Google* for sure because digital marketing is the norm now and Google leads the way.

Facebook

I am a Facebook user for one reason. It really helps me keep tabs on my friends and family. They are spread out all over the world and it's the most convenient way to keep appraised of what they are doing other than their annual Christmas letter.

There is a lot to not like about Facebook and that would mostly be the clutter and their ability to profile me. After all, Facebook must make money and they do that fine by understanding its members by what interests each one has and the member profile. In addition to the posts from friends and family, I get a lot of junk posts that are advertisers trying to reach me. I don't get overrun by them and I really find it amusing the posts that has a headline like: "Everything was going smoothly for this male model until this happened" or, "Hanging on the edge of the cliff with her life in peril, this mother of 8 had this happen." The not so subtle stories have some real content but only after going through 10-20 pages of lots of advertisements. Its bewildering but must be effective.

However, back to the story. Facebook deployed the elements of the *Hassle Quotient* and may not have realized it, but it is simple common sense. Make a consumer spend less time, use less effort, cost less (how about no cost?), and provide a superior experience and you have the magic formula. And if you do them all, the marketing will become viral.

I'm not saying Facebook doesn't have its issues and the admission that it did play an unwilling role in the 2016 federal election didn't help its position, but recently Facebook came out and stated they were going to lean back toward its roots of social posts and less news stories.

eBay

eBay started in 1995 as an online marketplace to match buyer and seller of items, both new and used. It really transformed the way used items were sold. In the late 1990's, the founders of eBay brought in Meg Whitman who inspired the vision of connecting people rather than just a platform for buying and selling items. Her vision led eBay to transition from a mainstay site for listing and selling collectibles to having merchants operate full on-line stores.

Before eBay, there were a couple of options to sell quality used items. Those included listing items in the classified section of your local newspaper, conducting a yard or garage sale, or placing a for sale sign on an item and trying to display it in a prominent location.

eBay started as an online auction. They made it simple and easy to list an item and even easier for prospective buyers to bid on items. Like Amazon, they have a powerful search engine to save time for anyone looking for items. Also, because of its marketplace approach, encourages intense competition between sellers so that buyers are assured of good value when selecting what to pay for items. Also, like Amazon, they enable feedback for both buyer and seller alike.

Probably the biggest criticism of eBay is that they don't get involved with shipping. Yes, they can help their eBay merchants with discounts for UPS, FedEx and Post Office, they don't offer much help when it comes to shipping larger-than-parcel items. They have partnered with uShip to have them assist with shipping estimates for cars, but largely haven't gotten involved with this critical part of the overall experience and I believe that has diminished the possible experience for a buyer.

In fact, uShip used to have thousands, if not millions of quotes on its platform for eBay buyers to determine the potential cost of shipping so they could be better educated on price bids. Merchants have adapted and learned how to quote up front on many items now, but large item shipping is still a challenge.

Craigslist

In today's world, if someone is interested in buying a used item, they are more likely to visit Craig's List than they are eBay. If there is a used item on eBay that one wants, you must wait until the auction has run its course unless there is a "buy it now" option. With Craigslist the item is typically immediately available unless the seller forgot to erase the item once it was sold.

Craigslist is also free for both buyer and seller and only charges for job postings in limited cities, and apartment listings in New York. Craigslist is not profitable and their President, Jim Buckmaster has stated he is more interested in providing a superior user experience to making money at this juncture. In 2010, Craigslist was estimated to be worth $400 million. I'm sure that value is now close to or over a billion dollars. Why? It's because Craigslist has created an efficient, easy way for buyers and sellers to connect to transact on used items. It draws immense traffic and meets all the criteria for have a superior Hassle Quotient than any other platform or method.

Craigslist doesn't have the most robust search engine, like an Amazon or eBay, but it has segregated its markets by geography so that buyers can more easily connect with sellers in their own backyard. That really helps with the shipping problem that eBay has. Regardless, I count Craigslist as a company that uses the Hassle Quotient formula as part of its entire strategy and dominates its space.

Monster/Indeed

It wasn't long ago when your local Sunday paper was about 3 times as thick as any week day publication. Was it that there was more news on Saturday and Saturday night that caused additional pages of stories? No, it was because of more inserts of ads but mostly because the classifieds were the most prominent part of the newspaper. On Sunday, the classified ads, would consume pages upon pages upon pages and the number one classified ad was for job opportunities.

Back then, it wasn't unusual for a company in need of talent to spend thousands of dollars for a single ad, especially if they wanted the ad to stand out amongst other ads. If they purchased a large ad, they could get more eyeballs on their ad and hopefully attract the right talent. Have you seen the most recent classified ads in our local paper? It is nothing like it was and there are very few jobs posted, nor items listed for sale. It's all gone online?

The most dominant job posting site is Monster.com who started back in 1994 which was in the pioneering days of the internet. Today, you will find over one million job postings and one million resumes posted on its platform at any one time. Nothing totally revolutionary here, and it doesn't have to be revolutionary to be dominant. It must save customers time, effort and money while providing a better experience than other options. Check the box on all those facets.

Like the others, Monster has a powerful and flexible search engine with multiple filters to enable job seekers to find openings that match their experience, location desires, functions and compensation needs. It is far less expensive for employers to post on Monster than to do the same the old-fashioned hard-print newspaper method.

However, there is one part of the experience that isn't ideal. Job seekers can apply to any job posting and employers must sort through massive numbers of resumes to find candidates that are truly qualified. Some companies have resorted to employing software to help sort through resumes looking for certain key words.

LinkedIn is another method that is highly effective for both employers and job seekers. This online professional networking platform enables recruiters and human resource staffing to refine searches and laser-like target qualified candidates or get referrals to source best candidates. And for job seekers, there is no better way than to network to find their best opportunities.

When the company "Indeed" launched its job search engine in late 2004, there was already plenty of competition in the space from well-established and well-funded companies like Monster and CareerBuilder. With that in mind, Indeed decided to use the resources it had — the company raised a single $5 million round in 2005 — to compete on product rather than marketing.

When Indeed launched in 2004, Monster, a main competitor spent $250 million on advertising that year, according to Rony Kahan, Indeed's CEO and co-founder. Kahan said "The only way were going to be able compete with Monster being bootstrapped was to provide a product that is 10x better." That thinking has continued up until the present: As Kahan said, Indeed has "never done any consumer brand advertising."

Indeed's innovative idea was to apply the "Google search model" for job listings. Rather than only show paid listings, Indeed crawls other job boards and company career pages to get a comprehensive selection of job openings by industry, location or keyword. This is an excellent example of reducing the amount of effort for a job seeker. It's also a testimonial to providing an outstanding customer experience and allowing viral marketing to make an impact.

While that strategy hasn't exactly helped Indeed to become as much of a household name as some of its competitors, it has nonetheless proven effective for attracting users to the site.

Indeed first passed Monster to become the top site for job search activity in the U.S. in 2010, according to comScore, and now has almost as many unique visitors in the job search category as Monster and CareerBuilder combined. Recently Indeed reached the milestone of 100 million monthly users and did it with minimal advertising. It's about on par with Instagram.

That is notable as its primary competitors, Monster and Career Builder have continued to advertise heavily including Super Bowl ads and year-round commercials and print ads.

With its huge success, Indeed got acquired by Recruit Co., a Japanese company. Even with the added resources available by Recruit, there likely aren't plans to buy a super bowl ad when the viral marketing of Indeed works so well. It proves the point that if you provide a better customer experience, save time and effort, customers will help spread the word. Thus, without a huge marketing budget, Indeed can charge less and make more money.

Match.com

Okay, I am admitting that I am not a customer, nor have I ever registered to be a customer of Match.com. I am blessed to have an awesome partner and never have had and hope to never need the services of Match.com. However, I have met many single folks who are looking for relationships, whether short-term or long-term and the alternatives to an online platform seem daunting. Many don't want to do the bar scene, and church has limited potential partners and other social venues might not cut it. Of course, you can depend upon your friends and family, right?

Again, I don't' know of their experience, cost or time and effort requirements but because they dominate this space, I assume they have it down, especially compared to non-online options.

By now I hope you are getting my point. Save your customers time, effort, money and give them a better experience than other options and you will dominate your space. Yes, it helps to be a first-mover but even if not, find the weakness of your competitor, know your desired customer and execute the heck out of it and you will win.

There are many examples of companies who have adopted the *Hassle Quotient* as their beacon to focus on the customer first and engineer itself backward. By doing this, these companies capture market share that result in significant market valuations for the companies. Once they get traction, there tend to be copy cats and important to always stay focused on the customer and continue to innovate to either reduce the time it takes to engage your company, reduce the amount of effort, find ways to become more efficient to lower prices and constantly make the user experience better.

GEICO Insurance

I am not a customer of GEICO, but their ads say it all. "You're here to save money and 15 minutes could save you 15% or more." I think shopping car insurance is a dreadful experience. It's time-consuming, confusing with lots of options and requires lots of effort. The user experience runs the gamut and I can't speak to the Geico experience, but they are appealing to me, the one without a lot of time and someone who wants to save money on a necessity, but something of a commodity. They are alike, right?

GEICO has a strong online presence and I can start the process online at my convenience. But they are appealing to the *Hassle Quotient* by promising me to minimize the amount of time it takes to engage them and to save me money. I assume the effort isn't herculean if it only takes 15 minutes and the user experience is seen as better just because it takes less time. Again, I am not a customer so can't claim the user experience is better, but I love how Geico incorporates the elements of the Hassle Quotient into their ads.

Chapter 6 - The Old Guard

I've been in the shipping, transportation and logistics industry practically my entire career. That career has now spanned 40 years. I have always found it fascinating how a package, pallet or full load can be in New York one day and just a few days later be delivered in Los Angeles. It's not just the physical movement of the freight that amazes me but the coordination of people and information that needs to take place to make that happen. It's especially true in the Less Than (truck)Load (LTL) and small package sectors as shipments needs to be merged with other shipments and loaded and unloaded a few times, sorted and routed to the right destination to hit a specific transit time. It's very interesting to me.

I have a lot of experience in the LTL segment of the transportation industry. Think about LTL as transporting palletized and crated shipments between buyers and sellers of products. This sector of the industry fits between the small package shipping world dominated by UPS, FedEx and the Post Office and full truckload shipments that you see on most every highway.

I spent twelve years within the Yellow Freight organization that now is known as YRC Freight. I was provided many opportunities to experience many facets of the business and met so many wonderful people along the way. It's a tough business, requiring a lot of coordination, technology and long hours. I love trucking as it really does drive commerce.

Look around the room right now and I can ensure you that everything you see, at one time or another, was transported on a truck.

The LTL industry is a long-standing one started back in the early 1900's. Even though the industry started as a regulated one, it went through deregulation in 1981 and yet, still maintains practices from the 1930's. If there was ever an industry that did not practice the tenets of the *Hassle Quotient*, the LTL industry is one. It takes a lot of time and effort to engage an LTL carrier unless you are a manufacturing or distribution company that ships and/or receives LTL daily. Pricing of LTL is extremely complex with substantial variations between customers and the overall experience is complicated and confusing to the non-informed. While UPS, FedEx and USPS have their own nuances, the small package industry is, by far, a much easier, simpler, faster industry to grasp and engage with a better user experience.

Prior to 1981, the industry was regulated by the former Interstate Commerce Commission. Carriers were restricted to certain territories or geographies they could service, and pricing was set by the ICC so basically carriers competed based on service performance. Competition was limited, and it was extremely rare to have a new entrant into any market as incumbent carriers could essentially block new carriers from entering their service territory. There weren't truckload carriers to any extent as that traffic was handled by LTL carriers.

Carriers expanded service territory mostly by acquiring carriers who had the authority to service specific territory. While a carrier could apply to the ICC for authority in a specific lane, any incumbent could protest and would likely result in the authority application being denied. Carriers provided costing data to the ICC to support the rates they charged. There were multiple entities called pricing bureaus that established rates by region of the country. The job of the rate bureau was to set rates based on carrier costs to ensure the carriers could operate profitably. The assumption was that it was more expensive to operate in the Rocky Mountains, for example, than in the southeastern part of the country. Pricing was not at all market-driven, but cost based.

Carriers made decent profits, provided an okay service, but pricing to the customer was strictly controlled by the ICC. The industry wasn't exactly a monopoly, but not a free market either. In 1981, the industry deregulated which allowed for carriers to service any locations and lanes and charge what they wanted to charge. At first, carriers focused on adding new territories, and given that pricing structures were complicated, didn't see the need to tackle price differentiation. The leadership of LTL carriers thought they could dramatically increase revenues and profit by extending service territories. It was years later that they started to undertake price differentiation.

One of the largest LTL barriers to adopting the *Hassle Quotient* is due to the complicated pricing structures that have been used since the 1930s and continue yet today. LTL carriers use a zip code by zip code matrix, typically three-digit zip codes with some five-digit zip code exceptions. However, the pricing isn't reciprocal due to lane imbalances. Let me give you an example. The price from Atlanta, say zip code 302, to Miami zip code 331 is going to be different than pricing from Miami 331 to Atlanta 302. The reason for that is that Miami is a consumption market with more shipments coming into Miami than coming out of Miami and thus, LTL carriers charge a premium for inbound Florida and provide lower rates for outbound Florida. In the regulated days, rate bureaus understood that dynamic and accounted for it in their rate base, even though one carrier's imbalance might be more significant than another.

LTL carrier rates are based on a price per hundred pounds or hundredweight. They use nine different weight categories, or breaks, and apply a different rate per hundred pounds for each. For example, they have a minimum charge, a rate for less than 500 pounds, more than 500 pounds, more than 1,000 pounds, more than 2,000 pounds, more than 5,000 pounds, more than 10,000 pounds and more than 20,000 pounds. The logic is that the heavier the shipment, the more efficient a carrier can be and thus lower the rate for heavier shipments.

Thirdly, LTL carriers use commodity classifications to price shipments. Commodity classifications are set by the carriers and are supposed to reflect the value of the commodity, the density of the commodity, the stow-ability and handling characteristics. There are 18 commodity classifications ranging from class 50 to class 500 and there is no symmetry.

It goes class 50, 55, 60, 65, 70, 77.5, 85, 92.5, 100, etc. Class 50 shipments are supposed to be low value, highly dense and easy to handle and stack. Think about a pallet of boxes of nuts and bolts. It is heavy, stacks easily and relatively low value. On the other hand, you can think about lamp shades that are not packaged. They are light, more valuable per pound and hard to handle and stack. Those might be class 400. In reality, there are very few class 50 and 500 classifications.

These classes are all spelled out in the National Motor Freight Classification guide. It's about the same thickness of an old Chicago telephone book and not only contains descriptions of practically every durable good and its corresponding classification, but also contains rules about packaging guidelines for shippers to ensure shippers abide by minimum packaging requirements to protect the contents of their shipments. The NMFC guide and contents is determined by the National Motor Freight Transportation Association. Basically, it is a bunch of carrier representatives who determine classifications. Shippers can submit for changes, but it is entirely up to this carrier group to make the call.

This commodity classification system was adopted by trucking companies back in 1935 as the railroads used it to help them price the transport of various commodities. It is still in use today though there is more and more momentum to adopting a density-based pricing system since more and more commodities in the NMFC are classed based on density. Just one example of how hard change is in the LTL industry. But the classification system is not easy for anyone to use and understand. It's subjective and cause for corrections by the carriers with additional charges being assessed to shippers.

In summary, you have non-reciprocal zip code pairs, 9 weight breaks applied against 18 commodity classifications to determine the base rate for an LTL shipment. It isn't even easy to print a rate sheet given the number of variables. It takes a computer to calculate rates. And I almost forgot, given the weight breaks, the LTL industry does allow for deficit weight rating. Basically, if a shipper has a shipment that almost weighs the next weight increment, say 990 pounds, the carriers will artificially increase the weight of the shipment to 1,000 pounds (the next weight break) so you can take advantage of the lower rate per hundred pounds and ultimately lowers the total cost of the shipment. That is one of the very few breaks a carrier provides.

Following deregulation, and once carriers were satisfied with their "land grab", the carriers started manipulating prices via discount incentives. At the time, I was working at Yellow Freight who was the first to offer an incentive called the YES discount. Basically, they provided a 12% discount if a shipper on a single day from a single shipping address tendered more than one shipment. The carriers reasoned that multiple shipments tendered at one-time resulted in pick-up efficiencies and could pass along savings to the shipper.

Naturally, that simple discount program was copied by competitive carriers and, before long, those efficiency-causing discounts turned into marketing discounts largely based on the promise of volume. It wasn't long before discounts were in the 80th percentile range and I've even heard of some 90% discounts. I joke that it's the only industry I can think of with average discounts in the 80% range without a "Going Out of Business" sign to accompany it.

But it gets better. Over time, the more sophisticated LTL carriers started to create their own prices called tariffs. They no longer needed to rely upon rate bureaus to set prices for them. They could set prices on their own and account for lane imbalances and operating costs they experienced and recover fees to cover those costs. Before this transpired, it was quite easy for a shipper to compare prices between carriers, even when they offered discounts. A 15% discount with carrier A was equivalent to a 15% discount with carrier B. Once the larger and more sophisticated carriers created their own proprietary base rates, it became impossible for a shipper to compare pricing without the help of a computer. Basically, with proprietary base rates and various discounts, one needs to compare the net charge from each pricing agreement to determine the lowest cost option.

With the complexity of pricing increasing, this would have been an ideal time that a progressive LTL carrier, or a start up to step in and transform the industry. Instead of requiring a customer to exert more effort, more time and more expense to simply get a rate up front, the LTL carriers made it more difficult. But, the changes didn't go unnoticed, nor addressed, but it wasn't addressed by the LTL carriers themselves, but by an entirely different industry. But before I go there, let's explore how LTL carriers have continued to make doing business with them harder, less convenient, and providing a less-than-ideal experience.

In addition to base rates, LTL carriers have a plethora of additional charges and surcharges. These additional charges are all spelled out in what they call their "rules tariff". These rules are typically found somewhere on their website and range from 50 pages for the simpler versions to over 200 pages for the larger carriers who offer a wider array of services. As services expand for a carrier, they apply rules which basically state what they will and won't do, and the circumstances for when they apply additional charges.

I won't bore you with 200 pages of rules that LTL carriers apply but want to point out a few. Within a carrier's rules tariff they stipulate charges for requiring a lift gate for delivery, for the additional charges of delivering to a residence, for delivering inside a building (something they state as not being immediately adjacent to the delivery truck), for delivering to a specified appointment, and for calling ahead before delivery. Most delivery modes want to know the phone number of the delivering party to arrange to spend less time delivering. For LTL carriers, they want to charge for calling in advance.

In the rules tariff, they also stipulate their fuel surcharges. Fuel surcharges started back in the days of regulation, in the early 70's when Arab countries placed an embargo on oil for the United States. At that time, fuel costs escalated rapidly, and trucking adopted a mechanism to account for the volatility of oil prices. It made sense and still does. However, the dirty little secret is that fuel surcharges for LTL carriers are a profit center. They make money at fuel surcharges and that is why they have resisted, to date, to adjust the formula. At about $1.10 - $1.15 per gallon of diesel fuel, the surcharges kick in and are generally applied as a percentage charge of net charges. Thus, if you are a shipper with a lower net charge based on discount, you pay less of a fuel surcharge than your fellow LTL shipper who hasn't negotiated as well as you. I have gone through the calculations of fuel costs, average payloads and determined that fuel surcharges are profit centers and the LTL carriers are not going to adjust the formula and start the scale at say $2.00 per gallon. When do you think diesel fuel is ever going to reach $1.15 per gallon? That's right. Never.

You see, LTL carriers admit that they aren't very disciplined with their base pricing and get leveraged to constantly increase discount percentages. With fuel and many other surcharges and accessorial charges, they don't get negotiated as much so they must have them in place to generate sufficient profit. As an example, in recent years, the LTL carriers have implemented flat rate surcharges for certain zip codes in higher cost delivery areas such as the loop in downtown Chicago, or the Burroughs of New York. Why don't they simply increase the base rate for those zip codes? Because they likely would discount those away.

Some of the more arcane rules LTL carrier deploy are for deliveries to what they call limited access points. Churches, schools, self-storage units, farms, golf courses and marinas are included in those lists. Even though they are businesses, LTL carriers claim they experience higher costs, largely because they don't have loading or unloading docks. However, they provide service to retail stores in strip centers and those are not considered limited access. LTL carriers also have rules about linear foot rules as they charge differently (more) for shipments that occupy so much linear feet in a trailer. Same thing happens when a shipper tenders a shipment being greater than 750 cubic feet in a single shipment that averages less than 6 pounds per cubic foot. They have rules for sorting and segregating, storage of goods, multiple delivery attempts, inside delivery (they are not UPS or FedEx) and many more.

On average, a shipper can expect to see a variance in about 30% of their invoices to what they might have expected to pay. The largest cause of corrected invoices by LTL carriers has to do with correcting the shipper's stated weight or commodity classification on the bill of lading created by a shipper. LTL carriers typically have a small error factor they allow, basically stating that unless the weight change is significant to go through the exercise, it's not worth issuing a new invoice. Sometimes that is stated in a weight amount, percentage of change in weight or even a dollar amount. What is notable however, is that LTL carriers charge a fee, like an administrative fee, for having to correct an invoice. It's like a fine and can range from $25-$40 for correcting weights. And now, most every carrier has a scale built into their forklift, so every shipment is weighed.

Same thing applies on changes to in commodity classification changes. If a shipper states they are shipping computers but failed to release a carrier's liability to $5.00 per pound, then they likely will face a higher classification and thus a higher charge per hundred pounds. Penalties apply for these changes just like weight changes. As more and more shipments are changing to density-based classes, it's up to shippers to accurately measure and weigh shipments to determine the density of each shipment. More and more carriers are deploying devices that quickly measure the dimensions of pallets or shipments while being weighed so they can more quickly correct a bill.

LTL carriers often boast about the millions of dollars they recover each year by weighing and inspecting shipments. All too often, the LTL carrier's attitude is that shippers are trying to cheat them, and they police it and penalize the abusers. Actually, shippers want to provide accurate information, so they know in advance, what their freight charges are. Many shippers charge their clients for shipping and handling and over 30% of the time, get an unexpected additional charge that they can't pass along to their client as they have already billed for shipping and handling. And, LTL carriers could use these discrepancies as an opportunity to work with shippers to avoid these charges and endear themselves to shippers, but they fail to do that.

There is an entire industry of freight bill audit and payment that has sprung up simply to deal with the complexities of LTL pricing, dispute resolution and payment. As you can tell, the LTL industry is ripe for transformation. Multiple carriers have tried to implement new processes as options but never gone to the extent of forcing any change that makes it simpler on shippers. They are afraid that their key customers will resist the change and shift business to a competitor. Fear, and fear of change is rampant in this industry.

While LTL carriers have been slow and hesitant to transform themselves, another new industry developed to take advantage of the high *Hassle Quotient* imposed by LTL carriers. That industry is known as 3rd Party Logistics. I think this is an outstanding case study of a start-up industry that takes advantage of a sub-industry that has failed to recognize the importance of the *Hassle Quotient* and paved the way for an industry projected to be a $1.1 trillion industry, yes with a "t", by 2024. That isn't all LTL but a portion of it is. There are other transgressors in the transportation space.

How does this story end? Did a new entrant come into the market and adopt the *Hassle Quotient?* Did an LTL carrier start and fundamentally make the user experience better, lower costs, require customers less time to engage and minimize the effort to navigate the complexities. The answer is: sort of.

No LTL carrier has emerged and changed the rules. While new carriers have emerged, many using an asset-light or non-asset model, they all have still adopted the old complex pricing practices, the hard-to-understand rules and are hard to engage. What has emerged, however, is an industry known as 3rd party logistics.

Prior to deregulation, carriers essentially charged the same rates. It was much like your utilities, you get a monthly bill and really have no basis for contesting it, so you pay it. Same thing in LTL. However, a few years after deregulation, LTL carriers started developing their own proprietary pricing models and then discounting off those complex rates began. It essentially became impossible for a shipper to discern the lowest cost carrier or rate without the help of a rate-shopping platform.

However, LTL carriers didn't have, and still don't, any interest in providing rate-shopping technology to their customers. Yes, they will provide tools to decipher their own rates, but don't want to expose competitive rates that might be cheaper. After all, United Airlines doesn't provide such fare-shopping software, why should an LTL carrier?

As LTL carriers diversified their rates, it was an opportunity for someone to step up and provide shippers what they needed. When LTL pricing started differing by carriers, the first LTL transportation management software systems were developed specifically to provide net rate quotes from multiple LTL carriers, or rate shopping. The first iterations of the TMS were quite expensive and only very large manufacturers and distributors could afford them. Due to the expense, some enterprising people started third-party logistics companies specifically to license the expensive TMS software and leverage that technology platform for many shippers. By taking the cost and applying it across many customers, the cost per customer was more reasonable. These early 3PL companies seized on an opportunity that the LTL carriers created and failed to solve for their shippers. The 3PLs took the complexity out of the problem, while enabling a better user experience.

Over time, 3PLs added integrations with multiple carriers so they could electronically tender shipments to multiple LTL carriers, could track and trace shipments through a single platform and could manage audit using the rating technology contained within the TMS. As a side note, the LTL industry spawned the freight bill and audit payment industry. It was created due to the complexity of the LTL rating process and the propensity for rating errors. It's just another example of an industry that has injected complexity into their offering forcing customers to spend extra time and effort to manage it, and a less-than-desirable user experience.

From the early days of simply providing a transportation management software for rate-shopping, the 3PL industry has evolved to helping customers negotiate contracts with LTL carriers. Yet, the pricing schemes are so complex, the average shipper doesn't understand all the nuances of the tariffs and rules LTL carriers can apply. It's almost like the tax code, where you hire a CPA to understand all the rules.

Some 30 years later, a very large industry has emerged. When counting global forwarding, a cousin to pure third-party logistics, the industry is expected to top $1.1 trillion in revenue by 2024. Just counting, the amount of LTL being managed by third parties is a staggering 35% of all LTL, or roughly $15 billion worth of LTL shipping.

Third party logistics companies help in lots of areas. They help their customers with claims, manage truckload movements, international shipping, fulfillment and everything in between. They provide in depth reporting and support and proactive tracking and problem resolution. They have become a single source solution for all aspects of logistics. They have embraced the *Hassle Quotient* by taking time and effort out of managing logistics, have lowered the shipping costs with astute carrier negotiation and they provide an overall better user experience by bearing the brunt of the complexity and making it simple for the customer or shipper.

For LTL carriers, they are slowing becoming more of a wholesaler. They are producing margins of at least $2.25 billion for managing LTL and that money could have been left in the LTL carrier's pocket had they recognized the need for making the customer experience simpler, taking time and effort out of the experience and reducing their costs.

Since we are on the subject of logistics, let's look at small package carriers. Most may not be familiar with LTL, but almost everyone is familiar with either UPS, FedEx the Post Office or all three. UPS was highlighted in the book, The *Discipline of Market Leaders*. Since I, at one time, worked for United Parcel Service, I can attest to their operational efficiency. They are the best of the best when it comes to engineering transportation operations. There are none better. FedEx? Never worked for them but I believe they operate the most efficient airline in the world. When you absolutely, positively want it overnight, right? And many joke about the Post Office, but they do a remarkable job delivering to every address in the United States, every day. No one else can boast that and they do it at ridiculously low rates. No wonder they lose billions of dollars each year, but I digress.

Because we all use small package services, we would think that one might be dominant, but that isn't the case. While their pricing seems to be relatively simple, for the business shipper it's not. They all have a convenience element to them, especially with the development of UPS Stores and FedEx Office locations spread around major cities. And we all know about our local post office, right?

Let's evaluate UPS first by evaluating the elements of the Hassle Quotient. For the average consumer, UPS, especially with their UPS Store outlets save time and effort. You can take your package, or even an unpackaged item, and they will box it, weigh it, measure it and determine your cost and you can pay on the spot with a credit card. They will give you a receipt with a tracking ID and even send emails as the package progresses. They will give you multiple options for transit time and it's relatively easy to get information from their website.

However, for the business shipper, there are elements of the LTL industry, meaning there are ample complexities, even though their pricing format is simpler due to its zone and weight scheme. Unlike LTL, UPS and FedEx, for that matter, have contracts with teeth to them. In other words, UPS and FedEx require volume commitments in exchange for pricing discounts. If you don't provide the specified volume, they penalize shippers with lower discounts. That seems reasonable. However, over the years, UPS and FedEx have both added many different surcharges and complications to their pricing. They have become more expensive than the Post Office, so they don't lead on price, but the user experience is also less than ideal for the business shipper.

UPS and FedEx, who are essentially carbon copies of each other, have implemented dim factors for each package over the past few years. Dim factors are used to determine the size of a package and to ensure that the carrier is compensated for the space the package takes, regardless of the weight of the package. Think of it this way, if you are shipping a lamp shade, it is probably a decent-sized box but weighs very little. In the old days, package carriers based their rates on weight only and therefore those who shipped lamp shades took more space than a nuts and bolts shipper yet were charged less. While that seems fair for the carriers, shippers now must measure each package to determine if the dim factor applies. The carriers also measure each package and issue corrections for packages not accurately measured. It takes more time for shippers to measure and more effort to evaluate, fight when necessary, and pay corrections.

The package carriers also, over time, began charging for deliveries to more rural locations with the creation of delivery area surcharges and extended delivery area surcharges. The rationale of the package carriers is that it costs more to deliver and pickup in less populated areas and therefore being compensated is reasonable. I get that but my hometown, one of about 20,000 people, with a UPS center in the town assesses a delivery area surcharge for every zip code in town. The small package carriers also charge for residential deliveries, charge extra if something is shipped not in a corrugated container, have fuel surcharges, though much less than LTL carriers, surcharges for long dimensions, hazardous materials and address corrections. The latter has been interesting as it is known that an address correction can be charged even if changing the term "Street" to "Road".

One of the biggest issues with customer experience is their invoicing practices. For a shipper that ships a few hundred packages per day, they will receive an invoice with line item detail (box by box and added charge by added charge) either electronically or printed. The printed invoices can be over an inch thick and basically impossible to audit. There is suspicion that parcel carriers charge base rates one week and any corrections to a shipment the following week so that a shipper cannot tie a correction to the original shipment. Basically, shippers either hire an audit and payment firm to review and audit invoices or simply pay the invoiced amount.

Contracts are very complicated and both UPS and FedEx don't allow consultants or third parties to assist shippers with negotiations. That is a relatively new development that I find highly suspicious as consultants understand the contract complexities and can, like a good CPA, help navigate the tax code to help clients.

In summary, for the business shipper, the parcel companies provide a very good service picking up and delivering packages, but cost shippers time and effort to deal with their complex and surcharge-laden fees. They are not the lowest cost option, but because of their vast networks, offer decent value. But overall, the user experience, while good for tracking and reporting, the invoicing process really dampens the user experience.

Now let's evaluate the Post Office compared to the parcel carriers. They have a much simpler pricing scheme, a multitude of options and price below UPS and FedEx. Yes, some would say that isn't fair as they are subsidized by the government, and there is some truth to that, but the simplicity of their structure isn't regulated. For example, the Post Office doesn't measure packages to charge a dim factor. They charge by weight and some win (lamp shade shipper) and some lose (nuts and bolts shipper). They don't have delivery area or extended delivery area surcharges. They deliver every address in the nation at the same cost. They don't charge fuel surcharges, nor do they charge for residential deliveries or if something isn't shipped in cardboard.

They innovated flat rate shipping with their Priority Mail envelopes and boxes. Their tracking has radically improved and even UPS and FedEx partner with the Post Office for final mile services within their SurePost and SmartPost offerings. They do have limits on weight however as their infrastructure is geared around smaller packages that fit in mail boxes. One thing that hampers the Post Office with business shippers is their relative inability to make pickups when the business shipper wants them. Unless it is a large shipper, the post office can have the mail carrier pickup when delivering mail, or the shipper must drop off the packages at their local post office. This one convenience factor inhibits the post office from securing more business shippers, but other than that, the Post Office comes closer to adhering to the elements of the Hassle Quotient than do UPS and FedEx. Another inhibitor is the Post Office requires shippers to pay in advance by depositing funds with an approved technology provider like stamps.com, Endicia or Pitney Bowes.

However, none of the small package providers are dominant. When UPS makes a change, FedEx pretty much follows suit, and vice versa. The Post Office, in my opinion, scores the best when it comes to the *Hassle Quotient* formula, but they fail to require less effort when it comes to picking up packages from business shippers. If they ever opted to schedule pickups in the late afternoon to match what UPS and FedEx do, that would go a long way. They also need to provide a better user experience when charging for their services. Many shippers simply don't like to pay up front and prefer to pay on terms.

Since I've spent my career in transportation and logistics, I have more experience with companies in this space. There are so many that don't have any clue about making it easier for customers to do business. I won't go into great length on these but wanted to provide a few highlights.

I do not have a lot of experience dealing directly with the railroad companies but have some acquaintances who have. The term that typically pops up is "captive" shippers. For grain, coal, lumber and a few other commodities, the rail is the most practical method of transporting product. However, railroads are a bit like a monopoly as shippers might have only one carrier option. In these cases, their option is to move via another mode, such as truck or barge. Using a truck is faster and offers a nimbler service, there are load constraints when comparing what a truck can haul to a rail car. Barges can hold more product but time in transit and ability to deliver directly is a challenge.

The standing joke working with railroads is that there aren't rate negotiations, just acceptance of what the railroad tells you what your rates will be for the coming year.

I did have an opportunity to work with a railroad once as I was wanting to ship a farm combine from Kansas City to Pacific Northwest. It was a total hassle just to try and find someone to talk with and get a quote. It was even a bigger hassle to work through the logistics of loading, securing and unloading. Just a horrific experience all the way around. I consider railroads like I do utilities. They are monopolies and they don't have to follow the *Hassle Quotient* formula.

When I think about the Hassle Quotient and market domination, I think of a few industries that really could substantially change their business by adopting some of the theories of the Hassle Quotient.

Car dealers

Thinking about buying a new car sends shudders up my spine because I immediately conclude it is going to take nearly all day. I hate the "let me take this offer to my manager" back-and-forth game, but some people love it. I value my time far too much, but also want value when making a purchase. I also detest the document fees and other absurd extra costs and options the dealers throw into the mix. It is a dreadful experience that takes way too much time, and someone needs to transform this industry. Maybe Tesla will do that once they get production figured out.

Cable companies

Millions are "cutting the cord" and a host of alternative options are coming out because dealing with cable companies is a dreadful, time-consuming and requires a lot of effort. But, at least they are expensive. All too often cable companies are like monopolies, being the only game in town.

Time share companies

If you haven't had the experience, I'll leave it at this. Time-share companies flunk at every aspect of the Hassle Quotient. They get an "F" across the board. Takes way too much time, too much effort to figure out their contracts, they are expensive and terrible investments and the experience, even after buying one, is awful. You must go through a lot of motions just to book your time share. And no, there is no dominant time-share company.

I imagine you can come up with your own hit list of industries or companies that are ideal for transformation as they don't get it.

Chapter 7 -5 String Logistics Solutions

In the Spring of 1999 I read a Wall Street Journal article about a young college graduate who had founded furniture.com and was being wooed by various venture capital firms in Silicon Valley to invest in his company. The venture capital firms were in a bidding war according to the article. Yes, this was at the height of the dot com era before the first bubble burst. Billions of dollars were being invested in various dot com startups and what struck me was that in the case of furntirue.com, here was a very smart young man getting a multi-million-dollar investment but with no practical business operating experience, especially in the industry where he was seeking millions in investment, the furniture industry.

At that time, I was a twenty-year veteran in the transportation and logistics industry and had an idea to start an internet-centric third-party logistics company. Together with a couple of industry friends, we developed a business plan and decided to seek funding. If a fresh MBA grad could raise millions to start a business where he had no practical experience, our combined industry experience should warrant a similar investment, so we reasoned. What we thought would be easy, wasn't easy at all. However, interestingly, the business plan we put on paper never came to fruition, and years later what we envisioned became, and still is, a growing trend in the LTL industry. Note to self; first-mover advantage is only an advantage if it works!

Even though we had a plan and had the experience we quickly learned that we needed revenue and traction to get any investment. One day, out of the blue, I received a call from an industry friend who had gone to work for Fritz Companies, a large international transportation company. He was in their Chicago branch and stated, "My grandmother could route freight better than we can." My reply was "Oh? Tell me about that." That was our opening and we seized upon it and though it took a lot longer than we ever anticipated, once we got revenue flowing via this shipper, we were able to secure our initial Series A investment.

For those of you who watch Shark Tank, not many pre-revenue companies are successful in attracting a shark as an investor. They want to see revenue and solid growth to ensure that they will get a return on their investment. That's an important lesson for anyone looking to start up a company. It wasn't any different for us. I left my comfortable job at Yellow Freight in July 1999 and was seeking funding and ultimately trying to get Fritz to be my first client. Ultimately, in November, Fritz finally engaged us, and we started generating revenue. That was a long four-month period when we didn't know if the plan we put on paper would work and I had left a good job.

Ultimately, we grew the company relatively quickly but still had to make multiple adjustments to our business model. Reflecting, I personally made a lot of mistakes and it was much harder than I ever anticipated. We started about a year after frieghtquote.com started but our business model was different. Freightquote.com became ultra-successful and years later was acquired by the number one freight broker in the U.S., C.H. Robinson. They concentrated on LTL transactions and we focused on developing solutions targeting larger shippers. In fact, in the very early days we met with the founder of freightquote.com and he encouraged us to drop what we were doing and join them, but we declined. I think that was a good decision as I would have clashed with their founder, given his background in telecommunications, and mine in transportation. Freightquote.com became a big success and we didn't.

The experience of starting a new business, while very hard, taught me a lot of lessons and as I said earlier, one of the things I was very proud about was making the shipping of LTL simpler and easier. We had a very robust website that allowed shippers to engage and they didn't have to know anything about commodity classification. They only needed to know weight and dimensions and we converted it to class for the LTL carriers and so long as the weight and dimensions were correct, there weren't any corrections. We got some notoriety for that as we created an ad that showed the NMFC guide (about the size of a telephone book for a decent-sized city) and had it covering a toilet paper dispenser, kind of like the old days when a phone book might have been used for substitute toilet paper. The old LTL guard wasn't thrilled with us taking a shot at their way of doing business, but we had a lot of fun with it.

One of the bigger challenges I experienced was the difficulty hiring good sales people and I had to make multiple changes to that leadership position. I wound up hiring a gentleman who had worked for McKesson, the drug and health care company. He had some outstanding relationships, but most importantly, he introduced me to the "courier" industry. At that time, I was an LTL expert and that was the world I knew. I learned that the courier industry was very large and a highly fragmented segment of the transportation industry. The courier industry has evolved and largely has started to drop the "courier" moniker in favor of local and final mile as the word courier all too often connotates bicycle messengers or document runners. There are couriers who do have bicycles and runners in the larger metropolitan markets but also have many capabilities well beyond that as they operate cars, pickup trucks, cargo vans, straight trucks and tractor trailers and provide warehousing and fulfillment services.

Our head of sales secured our largest and most profitable account, Home Interiors and Gifts. Prior to our involvement, Home Interiors and Gifts was using LTL carriers to ship their product. Unfortunately, they are no longer in business, but at the time, they operated a home party planning business where a host would schedule a party at their house and sell items to decorate homes including things like candles, wall hangings, figurines, vases and such. After consumers purchased items they would be shipped to the Home Interiors representative who would personally deliver the items to the party host. Typically, on any given week, a shipment of 5-10 boxes would be sent from the Home Interiors distribution center in Dallas to hundreds of Home Interior representatives.

When I was early in my Yellow Freight career, working as an inbound dock supervisor, we would receive trailer loads of Home Interiors. Every shipment was a residential delivery and many out in the countryside. None of it was productive for an efficient LTL delivery operation. We had to make appointments, deliver to time windows and so we basically would call the ladies and make a lot of excuses on how it would take us days to get their delivery to them. We knew that by doing this, most ladies would opt to come to the terminal and pick it up. Not an ideal experience for the Home Interior representatives, but more profitable for Yellow.

At our 3PL, freightpro.com, we were successful in securing this business and taking it away from the LTL carriers. We created a pool distribution solution, meaning we would load truckload quantities from Dallas and deliver that to local and final mile carriers (couriers) who would make the final delivery. Often, we had to coordinate multiple courier stops on the truckload to make it efficient, but it worked out so that we were able to save Home Interiors roughly 20% compared to LTL carriers and we made nearly 25% margins. The best part is that the delivery experience for the Home Interior representatives was greatly improved as the couriers delivered everything to exact specifications of the representatives. In fact, over time, Home Interior representatives would give their garage door codes to the drivers to make it convenient for both parties. If the lady wasn't home, they opened the garage door, set the boxes inside and went on to their next delivery.

Without even knowing anything about the formula, we lowered the *Hassle Quotient* for Home Interiors. We saved them a lot of money, gave them a better delivery experience and saved them a lot of time and effort over the LTL method. However, after a couple of years of providing this solution, the internal transportation team at Home Interiors pleaded with management that they could provide the same solution internally without us and thus save Home Interior even more money. Ultimately, they succeeded but with a less robust solution, but more importantly, Home Interiors had grown to account for 75% of freightpro.com's business. We simply couldn't reduce our costs fast enough to account for the loss of this much business. Yes, we knew the perils of having a single customer account for so much business, but it was beyond our control. Ultimately, what was left of freightpro.com was merged with another company. However, and most importantly, the experience with local and final mile carriers left a lasting impression upon me. I knew that this highly fragmented sector of the industry could help other companies improve user experience at lower costs with a lot less effort, if, and a big if, there was a way to harness them.

The local and final mile industry is dominated by carriers who use independent contractors (IC) to provide the pickup and delivery service. The IC provides their own vehicle and can choose to work as much or little as they like. It's Uber, before Uber, only instead of transporting people, they transport shipments. They provide both on-demand and routed distribution work. On-demand works well for anyone needing something moved same-day across town where the routed work is used for repeat business where customers might send trailer loads of product to the carrier's facility, much like we did for Home Interiors and Gifts.

Due to their operating model, it doesn't require huge investments of capital though they do have to provide technology, buildings and often tractor trailers as ICs for that size equipment is harder to find. But from a cost perspective, leveraging carriers who use ICs can create a cost advantage as ICs cost less to operate than employees. ICs are paid a percentage of the revenue, in most cases, just like Uber. So, local and final mile companies can compete on price as they need to balance winning the business and yet paying an IC a rate that covers the cost of operating a vehicle and paying them a living wage.

Ever since my experience at freightpro.com I had been trying to figure out how engage this flexible, nimble and lower cost solution in companies in which I was engaged. However, I kept finding a way how to engage local and last mile carriers to be elusive. There are two associations that focus on local and final mile carriers. One is the Customized Logistics and Delivery Association (CLDA) and used to be called the Messenger and Courier Association of America but changed their name to de-emphasize messenger and courier as they were gravitating toward larger shipments and freight. The other association is the Express Carriers Association (ECA). What is interesting about ECA is they have an annual conference that is a speed dating event. For two days, shippers and carriers spend 15 minutes each to meet each other and quickly explore whether it makes sense to do business together. While productive, it can also be extremely confusing. There are approximately 7,000 local and final mile carriers in the United States. Working with these carriers is a bit like herding cats. Each carrier has its local or regional service territory, different operating system, no standard set of services, various pricing formats and is woefully under-represented by sales. As a shipper, one basically needs to know about these carriers and seek them out. I've attended many ECA conferences but getting them engaged afterward has been a challenge.

So, I did a lot of thinking and soul-searching about how to go about herding these cats. I wasn't sure. For years I had tried and failed but then I was asked to speak at an Air Cargo conference. I wasn't sure what to present and just started thinking about the most successful companies and what I thought really made them different. This is when I originally came up with the concept of the Hassle Quotient and presented it. Companies that dominate provide a service that requires a customer to spend less time and effort, costs less and yet, provides a superior experience. The key is a company cannot trade one off for the other. It's a formula that metrics can be inserted, so long as a company's customers are calculating those metrics. Granted, it was in rough form when I presented it but got me to thinking more about it and doing research.

It was shortly after that conference that I started thinking about the local and final mile industry in general and how I needed to apply the *Hassle Quotient* to make it easier for shippers to engage local and final mile carriers, enable them to engage them more efficiently so they spend less time and effort using them and then provide them an experience as good or better than other options. After all, final mile is a hot space with the growth of e-commerce. I am especially attracted to final mile services for "larger-than-parcel" services. If I could remove the hassle, the costs would be better for shippers and I knew the experience would be significantly better, especially when compared to LTL carriage, as we proved that at freightpro.com.

Those thoughts became the foundation for 5 String Logistics Solutions. First, I want to explain the name. Yes, it is a bit unusual. It came about as I play (or at least attempt to play) the 5-string banjo. I play it Earl Scruggs style, meaning I use the three-finger picking style that is so popular in bluegrass. You see, playing the banjo requires significant amount of coordination between both hands and the fingers on both hands. One hand and set of fingers control the fret board to suppress the right strings at the correct fret positions to result in the proper note being played. At the same time, the other hand must pluck the proper string that is properly fretted at the right time to produce music.

Without every finger and hand being synchronized and being coordinated perfectly, one will hear a lot of noise and not music. I know, some think a banjo can't produce music, but we'll save the jokes for later. The concept of the banjo is a perfect analogy for local and final mile carriers. Typically, there must be a first and perhaps middle mile to coordinate and synchronize with a final mile carrier to produce the desired results. With the coordination, late deliveries, missing or damage shipments might take place.

While I was trying to figure out how to herd the cats of local and final mile carriers, I started thinking about the Air Cargo conference presentation I made regarding the *Hassle Quotient* and that placed in motion a strategy to make it abundantly easy, simple and efficient to engage local and final mile carriers. I decided that I didn't want to be a third-party logistics company, as that would require additional margins to be added and not offer the lowest possible price. Third parties also choose a single partner provider per market and that might not work given the wide array of services local and last mile carriers provide. I also figured out how to develop a very efficient engagement to make the user experience as outstanding as possible.

My last job, before embarking upon the journey of founding 5 String Logistics Solutions, was with a company named uShip. For those not familiar, uShip is an online marketplace matching buyer and seller of shipping services. It works a bit like Orbitz or Travelocity where carriers can make themselves available online and shippers can engage carriers a variety of ways like seeking bids, making offers or accessing immediate published rates. uShip's core business is catering to consumers who need to ship large items yet are not sure how to go about it. uShip's largest categories including car shipping, boat shipping, motorcycle shipping and furniture shipping. I was brought aboard to help launch a marketplace offering targeting business shippers and elected to engage LTL carriers on the platform, since so many 3PLs were engaging in that mode of transport. If you've ever watched the television show *Shipping Wars*, that was produced to highlight uShip.

Over time, I was able to sign more than 30 LTL carriers to participate in our marketplace, and since LTL carriers don't engage in bidding or accepting offers, we wanted to expose their published rates that could change as the LTL carrier needed them to change. In other words, like airlines do, we wanted LTL carriers to be able to modify their pricing as the LTL carrier saw fit. If they had a lane needing additional traffic, they could price that more competitively than other lanes or other competitors. To accomplish that, we needed to set up quoting via Application Program Interface or API. This electronic integration protocol is much more nimble than conventional Electronic Data Interface (EDI) and there weren't any EDI transaction sets that support price quoting.

Being a technology company at its core, uShip had the option of setting up integrations with all thirty LTL carriers, one at a time. However, that would take an inordinate amount of time, effort and money. We elected to contract with Banyan Technology who operates an API hub technology platform. They are in the business of connecting trading partners using APIs as the mechanism and over years had connected to over 1,000 freight carriers. Through a single integration with Banyan we were able to connect electronically to our 30 plus carriers to enable real-time electronic quoting, push electronic booking with the carriers and then retrieve shipment status as the shipments were being moved about. We also were able to receive electronic invoices from our carriers but used conventional EDI to accomplish that.

APIs are important as many shippers and most all third-party logistics providers use Transportation Management Software (TMS) and want to engage their carriers electronically, much like we did at uShip. By connecting electronically, the engagement is much easier and eliminates the need to call carriers, access the carrier's website or send emails.

Given that the local and final mile industry is so fragmented, and like herding cats, I decided that it was important to enable electronic connection between shippers, 3PLs and other intermediaries to local and final mile carriers, and using API would be the preferred method. I then met with Banyan to find out if they had already connected to local and final mile carriers. After all, they had connected to over one thousand carriers, so maybe they had already done this. Turns out they had not connected local and final mile carriers and didn't know where to begin. I knew that local and final mile carriers are smaller, entrepreneurial companies after dealing with them for years. I knew that most of the time a local/final mile carrier engaged a software company that developed dispatch software for them.

Thus, I knew five of the major dispatch software vendors as I had been attending trade shows for years and met several of them. I contacted the top five dispatch software companies to learn their status on supporting APIs for quoting, booking and tracking. It turned out that each dispatch software company was in various phases of having published specs available. One of them had everything we needed, three of them could support pushing of orders and retrieving shipment status via API and one was just getting started with the programming. At that juncture, I went back to Banyan and told them that it wasn't a mature API environment but thought we had enough to get started. They agreed, and we executed an agreement whereby we would work together to bring the local and final mile world into the modern world of API capabilities.

Having been in the logistics and transportation industry for over 39 years, I had developed a pretty decent rolodex. I've had the good fortune of developing some great relationships and many of those were either working for LTL carriers or third-party logistics companies. I knew that the local and final mile carriers have limited sales bandwidth and were not reaching the contracts I had and who wanted to use their services. This void really instigated the creation of my company 5 String Logistics Solutions. However, I knew that all my contacts would require that any carrier relationship must be connected electronically, and thus the relationship with Banyan Technology was critical.

I decided that the easiest way to engage customers was to engage them with no obligations or cost on their part. The parties that would receive the most value were really the local and final mile carriers who I was representing and could connect via API. So, I decided to become a commissioned business development agent for local and final mile carriers who could electronically connect, though I wouldn't agree to being exclusive with any provider in a single market. I wanted to ensure that I had carriers who could provide whatever services the shipper or 3PL needed, the right type of vehicles, all the while ensuring that pricing would be competitive by providing the customer multiple options. I initially described that I was like a sports agent, manufacturer's rep or headhunter whereby I represented multiple athletes or executives. Some have since described what I do as a concierge service. Either way, I am helping shippers connect with local and final mile carriers who provide a variety of highly flexible services at very competitive rates.

Two important trends also drove my decision to start 5 String Logistics Solutions. One is that approximately 35% of all shippers have adopted a Transportation Management System (TMS) to manage all their shipping. Intermediaries, including 3PLs use a TMS 100% of the time. Anyone with a TMS resists engaging carriers manually so connecting via API is important if carriers want part of their business.

The other trend is that more and more shippers are engaging third party logistics providers to manage all their logistics and transportation. Armstrong and Associates, a highly respected consulting firm in the logistics industry projects that by 2022 $1.1. trillion of logistics expenditure would be managed by third parties, including forwarders on a global basis. The reason for that trend is that 3rd parties invest in the latest technologies, have skilled and experienced staff and know-how and can leverage volumes to generate efficiencies and cost savings. It is often more efficient for companies to engage 3PLs than to make the necessary investments on their own.

Now, with the limited sales staff of final mile carriers, they aren't making calls on third parties that can be anywhere in the world. They typically are calling on local companies but routing decisions more and more, are being made outside the city that the shipper resides. So, it really isn't practical for a local/final mile carrier to make the necessary sales calls for this category of shipper. Imagine a local carrier from Houston making a call on a third-party in Chicago and they ultimately ask if they have any work in Houston. No, but we do in Dallas! Sorry, we are only in Houston. Whereas, 5 String Logistics Solutions can make the same call and simply find out what needs they have and where and match them up. It's a win for the carrier and a win for the shipper. Plus, 5 String becomes a cost of sales for the carrier and on a variable basis only.

Let's review how 5 String has applied the principles of the *Hassle Quotient*. 5 String saves carriers time and effort as I leverage my rolodex, relationships and promote their services to prospects they aren't reaching. For shippers, 5 String saves them time and effort by connecting them to the right carrier in the right geography and services without having to do research and vet and qualify multiple providers. 5 String then enables direct relationships between the parties without adding a margin. 5 String becomes a cost of sales that a carrier would have to bear anyway. Thus, shippers are getting the very best market deals available. Finally, the experience is efficient both in the engagement process, but especially after they start doing business by connecting via API. Shippers can easily get quotes like they do from other carriers, book electronically, get shipment status electronically and even invoices.

While it is early in the life of 5 String, so far, the reception of the business model has been good, and prospects look great. I am committed to continue to refine my processes to make it easier and easier for both carriers and shippers to engage 5 String and each other.

Chapter 8 – Dominant Compared to Trade-Off Companies

As expressed in the book the *Discipline of Market Leaders*, the theory was that companies needed to focus on a single discipline to be considered a leader. That might have been true at that time, but times change and now, to be a dominant company, you must do it all. You must be all things to all people. You need to master all facets of the Hassle Quotient to dominate your market.

I admit it is a difficult thing to do. I think it's more difficult for existing companies to retrofit and set up a new culture than it is for a start-up. Right off the bat, some are thinking that to give a customer the best experience, it's going to cost more to provide that awesome experience and thus, we must price higher to get an adequate return on our investment. That might be true, and that might make one a good or great company, but not a dominant one. It's okay to be a good company. It's even better to be a great company. Nothing wrong with either of those. But, if you want to dominate your market, you must embrace, conquer, and solve the Hassle Quotient with all elements, as determined by your customers. It's not what you think and how you think you score using the Hassle Quotient, it's what your customers think.

There are a couple of dominant companies that come immediately to mind. The first is Amazon. They dominate the online shopping marketplace space. Any shopper can engage them and spend little time, exert little effort, get great prices and have a great overall experience. It's why they dominate, and it comes down to every single click of the mouse that counts.

Uber is a dominant company. They transformed how to get a ride, especially compared to conventional cabs. They engineered an experience that takes little time, exert little effort at a price far superior to cabs and a great customer experience.

Both Amazon and Uber have been richly rewarded with impressive market valuations for being dominant companies. However, being dominant doesn't mean you have to be internet-centric, or relatively new to be a dominant company. If you operate a local plumbing service, you can dominate your market, so long as you adhere to the covenants of the Hassle Quotient and engage your customers to understand how you stack up to other plumbing companies in your market. It is not easy to adopt the components of the Hassle Quotient and follow all of them, not trading off one for the other.

When you are a dominant company, you will be amazed at how viral marketing will help you capitalize on your position. You know, Amazon never employed a blimp to advertise nor did Uber advertise during the Super Bowl. I guess Amazon did advertise Alexa, but that was 2018 and up until then, they never needed to do that and reap their dominant position. They set up the formula and executed and then you know what? Their customers shared their experiences and recommended each company and they became household names.

Today, very few companies dominate their market. It's hard to break old habits. Those old habits involve trade-offs. It's what corporate America knows. Companies and managers tend to manage based on attaining certain financial goals and not on market share. That practice is time-tested and It's what makes entrepreneurs tick. Again, nothing wrong with it, but I would rather dominate than just be a good or great company.

Trade-Off Companies

I recently asked a shopping expert a couple of innocent questions as I didn't want to reveal the purpose of my questioning. That expert is my wife. I think any wife, or any person who enjoys shopping, is a credible source for what I call trade-off companies.

A trade-off company is one that isn't dominant but could be a good or great company. A trade-off company excels at all facets of the Hassle Quotient and doesn't trade customer experience for price, nor price for time and effort spent, etc. They provide it all.

So, the innocent question went like this. "Walmart or Target"? Without hesitation, she responded Target. Naturally, I had to ask why. First, I can't get a parking spot at Walmart, she responded. So, Walmart is more popular I stated. Maybe, but I can't always get what I am looking for at Walmart. Even though prices are slightly higher at Target, I can typically find what I am looking for, with more selections.

She wasn't done. I asked who had the better staffing. She immediately recanted a recent story where she electronically sent some photo files to have them developed into prints. Guess that is still a thing....printed copies. Anyway, she said she went back to the film desk and had to wait more than twenty minutes as there were two other people waiting in front of her. When she finally got to the associate, she gave her name and the clerk researched their system and couldn't find anything. The clerk summoned her supervisor to help as this clerk was filling in for the permanent person. The supervisor asked the name to which my wife replied "Bramlett" and immediately discovered the clerk used the name "Bradley" and the root cause of the problem.

My wife is under the assumption that Walmart just has people filling in wherever and not necessarily trained for any role.

She continued. She believes that Target is better organized, cleaner and brighter. I had to ask about the number of checkout lines and how many cashiers were typically working. Again, she favored Target. So, all in all, my favorite shopper prefers the overall experience of Target, the amount of time it takes to park, shop and checkout. She is willing to trade-off the higher prices she believes Target has for the time required, effort and overall experience.

If Target matched Walmart's price and let everyone know they did that, provided a better experience in everyone's mind, required less time and effort to shop, they likely would dominate the in-store general merchandise experience. Granted, my wife's perception of adequate parking might be a thing of the past if they became dominant, but then maybe they would implement valet parking. Don't you love how many downtown restaurants provide valet parking and you don't carry anything other than leftovers from a restaurant back to your car. In retail, you might be lugging several bags of groceries and must hike a half-acre to load your car. But I digress.

I asked my favorite expert shopper her impression of the three major grocery store chains in our vicinity. She adequately provided her opinion of each store's overall experience, pricing compared to each other and speed and effort to shop there. She alters her shopping with grocery stores depending upon what she needs. The new trend is home delivery of groceries. We recently tried that and with a minimum spend of $100, a local grocery store will shop for you and arrange a delivery to your specified time. Anymore, it really doesn't take much to accumulate $100 of groceries. When I think about the amount of time it takes to shop, it's a very good value. My only concern was the quality of produce. I confirmed with my daughter-in-law, a frequent home delivery customer, that the produce is the best because they do not want to risk losing a customer by delivering less-than-ideal produce.

My major point is that if you operate a company, you must understand your customer. Who is your ideal target? If you are a trade-off company and you wish to cater to the bargain shopper, then you need to focus on pricing and can trade-off the overall experience with time and effort required to shop there. Most importantly, you need to ask your customers about their impressions. What do they think about the time and effort you require of them. You need to ask about their overall experience. You need to ask about how your pricing stacks up. You need do this constantly because your competitors are not going to stand still. Even if you decide not to be a trade-off company and try to become a dominant company you need to stay appraised of your customer perceptions. Being dominant is hard. Heck, operating any kind of company is hard. You need to stay up with your changing customer's needs, understand their desires and fulfill those.

The way many companies try and stay in touch with customer opinions and experiences is to provide a survey. I recently visited the post office and there was a survey link at the bottom of my receipt and the clerk pointed that out to me. I've had the same experience at fast food restaurants, but of course, they use rewards like free sandwiches or discounts on my next visit.

There are a variety of questions companies ask in their surveys but let me give you the short and sweet best survey they use.

1) Compared to our competitors, how much time was required engaging us compared to our competitors?
2) How much effort did you have to exert to engage us compared to our competitors?
3) How do you find our prices compared to our competitors?
4) How would you rate your overall experience using us compared to our competitors?

5) What can we do to improve the overall experience we provide you?

Let me give you some other trade-off examples. Some of my favorites are examples of various airlines.

I'm a Southwest man when I fly. Yeah, I've tried most of the others and had good and bad (very bad) experiences, but more times than not, Southwest meets most of the components of the HQ. While they have become and are the largest domestic airline, they don't dominate. While they advertise low fares and many times they do have low fares, they are not the lowest cost option when booking last minute flights. I define last minute flights as booking air within a week of departure. I always seem to find lower fares on the other major airlines when I need last minute air travel.

Let's explore all the formula components a little closer. I like their website experience. They provide multiple options to review fares, but also easy navigation to other parts of their website to manage my account, check points in their loyalty program and check things like flight status. The amount of effort I must exert is minimal as I book everything online and they are priced very competitively, if not cheaper, when booking 2-3 weeks in advance.

Southwest really shines in two pricing areas. First, they don't charge for checked bags. That alone can take $50-100 off when comparing other fares. The bigger one, at least for me, is the ability to change my flight schedules without any change fees. I know some airlines charge as much as $200 to make a change to an itinerary. That amount sometimes surpasses the total fare by Southwest.

From an experience standpoint, there are a couple things that stand out. A couple are a bit controversial. First, there is no seat assignments. Some don't like that. I like it because, based on when I check in, I can choose to select where I want to sit. If I happen to see a screaming baby, I might just take a seat at the opposite end of the airplane. In fact, some airlines charge you based on the seat you want. I distinctly recall flying another airline and trying to move to an emergency row seat after the door had shut. It wasn't long before I was chased from that seat because I hadn't paid for that. Not allowing a paying customer to change seats when the seat is available, isn't a great experience in my opinion.

The second somewhat controversial point for Southwest is that they don't have first class seats. Now, many business travelers like to build various statuses and get an upgrade to first class where they get wider seats with more legroom, free drinks and snacks and priority boarding. Yes, it is a great experience, but that part of the experience isn't worth the trade-off of Southwest. I know that on one other airline I was in Boarding Group 2. Hey, I thought, that was a pretty good draw. Surely, I will get my carry on stored in the overhead compartment with that level of priority boarding. Well, after Diamond, Gold, Platinum, Super Dooper Purple and whatever other groups there were, 90% of fliers were aboard and couldn't get my bag in the overhead. I learned that they don't charge when you carry on and ultimately get it checked for free, so I had that going for me.

One of the other big differences in experience, is that Southwest has no blackout dates for their frequent flier program. If I have the points, I can fly whenever there is a seat available. And, their points don't expire where I have had other programs where they have expired.

Finally, and almost as important as everything else, I love the Southwest culture and the lighter attitude of their flight staff. They have fun and crack jokes and make the flying experience a bit better. I'm biased, but I think Southwest is more on-time than others and I personally, will drive 3 hours to take a Southwest flight if my other option is another airline.

American/Delta/United

Pick another airline like American, Delta or United. To me, they are all the same and operate hub and spoke systems that, unless you live in the hub city, requires most travelers to fly through the hub city. That always is a risk as those hub cities are typically large with flights coming and going every few seconds. Any small hiccup causes backups, delays and cancelled flights. Yes, I am talking about you Chicago, Atlanta and Dallas.

If you are a preferred flier, the experience is very different than for us average Joe's who take a flight from time to time on their airline. Yes, you can select your seat in advance, but only certain seats come at no extra cost. They specialize in finding ways to add additional revenue, whether that be your seat assignment, checking a bag or changing an itinerary. It's a bit of a gamble to know what you are going to pay for your service. And you would think that if you actually pay for your luggage to travel with you that it would. One would think it would take priority over checked bags, like when there could be an overweight aircraft issue, but it doesn't. My wife took a trip and found out her paid luggage didn't make the trip with her due to the potential of the aircraft being too heavy. I guess that's better than the alternative where someone boards the aircraft before taking off and saying "Attention, we are going to need to have all your free carry on luggage removed due to the potential of our aircraft being too heavy."

These airlines also work with multiple commuter airlines which means you get to fly in either regional jets or propeller airplanes. I'm a relatively big guy, those aircraft just don't suit me very well.

These airlines trade-off lower fares for very specific rules about advance bookings without change, flying with carry-on bags only and sitting wherever they say it is convenient for them. You get to board last and they will allow you to purchase food (sometimes) on their flights.

Allegiant/Spirit

There is a class of airline that promotes extremely low fares, but their customer experience is not up to par with the other airlines mentioned. During their booking process, the base fare may be low but it's not unusual to pay for the seat you want, pay for carry-on baggage, and pay for even a soft drink. They specialize in "nickel and diming" their customers. In fact, one or both charge higher fares if you must speak to one of their representatives. "Hey, that costs money!".

I recently booked a trip with Allegiant. They absolutely cater to the tourist or casual traveler as the airports they serve target popular vacationing spots such as Las Vegas and points in Florida. Therefore, their flights are not on a daily basis. They might depart a city on Thursday or Friday and return on Sunday or Monday. So, you must know you are going to travel on that day, that time and to that destination, else your changes are going to be major.

While booking my airfare with Allegiant, it was not a quick and efficient process. There were likely 10 different pages to navigate plus getting sold car rentals and hotels along the way. I recall that when I started the booking process, it stated there were limited seats available at that price. Really paid little attention to that. Well, by the time I got through their arduous, time-consuming booking process, at checkout I was told that there were no more fares available at that specified rate. Rats! Rather than retain all my information I had already entered, including credit card, their process took me back to the start of booking and had to re-enter everything all over again. All for a fare increase of about $4. Really?! Just not a good booking experience.

Again, great and good companies trade-off one or a couple components of the Hassle Quotient formula. It's fine but you cannot trade anything off and be a dominant company in your marketplace or industry.

Chapter 9 - Companies that Get It

You don't have to invent a new widget to start a new company. You don't have to disrupt an industry to launch the next big thing. Yes, you can transform an industry and do big things. You can also focus on taking an existing business and modifying the business so that your customers can engage you faster and easier than your competitors, price lower than your competitors and make the overall experience better than the experience your competitor provides.

Here are several companies, mostly newer in nature, that have taken the Hassle Quotient to heart. In fact, one of them is based 100% on the principles behind lowering the Hassle Quotient.

Freightquote.com

I have already detailed how difficult and complex the LTL industry is. However, it is an essential service for many businesses who deal in durable goods. They use LTL to bring in raw materials and use LTL to ship finished orders out. Freightquote.com was founded in 1998 just after the internet became a viable platform to conduct business. It took an outsider to the industry, a telecommunications executive named Tim Barton, to see the opportunity and seize upon it.

Back in 1998 approximately 60% of an LTL carrier's business would be under contract rates, meaning the shipper and carrier specified very specific terms and rates to apply to its business. The remainder or roughly 40% were agreements (not contracts) that specified rates that were higher than contract rates and many small businesses had neither a contract or a pricing agreement. LTL carriers provide pricing as a percentage off some obscure set of base rates that are difficult to compare. All too often shippers receive a discount but have no clue as to the actual base rate nor the net dollar charge until they received the invoice. Very customer unfriendly as it's like a proverbial blank check.

Mr. Barton had the idea to target the smaller shippers who didn't warrant very deep discounts and suffered through a less-than-delightful experience by not knowing what their charges were in advance of engaging an LTL carrier. He figured that he could attract a good volume of shippers by providing a better experience and then leverage the aggregate volume to both provide a better price to the shipper and at the same time scrape a margin while providing the service.

He modeled the user interface to reflect how travelers were able to shop and choose airfares through Orbitz, Expedia and Travelocity. In other words, a shipper could input basic parameters like the origin zip code, destination zip code, weight and class and multiple rates and anticipated transit times displayed, and the shipper could choose the one that suited them best, whether that be best price, carrier they liked the best or even expected days in transit. The shipper could pay by credit card, produce a bill of lading online, track a shipment through its lifecycle and later see reports and dashboards to reflect their shipping activity.

While LTL carriers initially resisted dealing with a middleman like freightquote.com, over time, the demand increased, and LTL carriers had to engage or simply lose a significant revenue opportunity. Freightquote.com was successful using a large inside sales team and grew to several hundred million dollars in top line revenue and multiple copycats spun off. Freightquote.com was a leader in transforming the transactional LTL industry and ultimately was purchased by C.H. Robinson, the world's largest freight broker.

It takes a shipper less time, uses less effort, produces a lower price point with a better user experience than dealing directly with any LTL carrier. That's it.

I think freightquote.com has enough clout that they could further simplify the engagement of LTL, but we shall see. If they can rid themselves of commodity classification and go with only requiring dimensions, that will simplify the process for shippers as well as result in fewer commodity classification corrections, lowering shipper costs, that would improve the experience.

As LTL carriers continue to increase surcharges for services such as residential delivery, inside delivery, and lift gate, there will come a day when shippers will want to combine LTL carriers for first and final mile while engaging a lower cost, more flexible provider (local and final mile carrier) for last mile.

Legacy Home Inspections

A very good friend and fraternity brother of mine started a home inspection business about four years ago named Legacy Home Inspections. Previously he had worked in sales for a large national company and later got into the seminar training business. So, when I met him for lunch four years ago and he told me he was starting a home inspection business, I was a bit surprised, but I knew nothing about the home inspection business and just wished him well.

I didn't keep up with Robert but recently had lunch once again to catch up and learned that he was now the largest home inspection company in Kansas City doing nearly 10 times more inspections than the average home inspection company. He was so successful in Kansas City, he was now franchising and already had franchises in St. Louis, Springfield and Wichita with plans for opening Denver. Des Moines and Atlanta.

Being the curious type, I asked Robert what his secret was. He immediately referenced his tag line "It's not about us." I love that as he recognizes it's all about serving the customer, the home buyer. He also has a nifty marketing strategy to become favored by realtors, but what struck me was how he makes it easier for home buyers than other home inspectors.

At Legacy Home Inspections, there is a guarantee the inspection is to be performed within 48 hours. That is a big deal as the home inspection process can really impact the price negotiation of the home and slow the closing down as repairs are based on the findings of the inspection. And if the inspection takes a while to complete, it is going to push back the necessary repairs and closing. Legacy also uses thermal cameras to identify where the house might be leaking cold air in the summer or hot air in the winter. Those cameras can also detect if there is a hidden problem in the breaker box (electric panel). Are those required in the home inspection process? No, they are extras that home buyers appreciate. Legacy also provides termite and radon inspections without having to coordinate other companies to do that. Again, that reduces the amount of coordination and time to complete the inspection process.

Finally, Legacy targets a price point 15% -50% below their competitors. Let's see, easier, faster, with better economics and an overall better experience? Yep, sounds like Legacy is on track to have a lower *Hassle Quotient* than their competitors and winning more customers and dominating.

There is always room for improvement however. I advised Robert that if he wanted to save time for home buyers to book his services, he should create a mobile app that a realtor could quickly access as realtors are about the most mobile workforce out there and when they have the buyer in the house and ready to write an offer or get an offer accepted, they could immediately book the inspection. Naturally, when they are ready, Legacy will need to engineer the mobile app to be simple and easy with as few pages as possible.

Another idea to investigate is to deploy an online calendar that allows users to schedule and book their own appointment. If Legacy has 10 inspectors than once ten appointments are booked, that time slot is no longer available. An interactive calendar would allow Legacy to be more efficient and allow customers to engage more quickly and by not talking with anyone. They would be able to book 24 hours a day.

Finally, with the emergence of APIs, I told Robert that he could use APIs to integrate his calendar and services into back-office applications that realty companies use. Again, make it simple for realtors to coordinate engaging Legacy and if Legacy is easier to book than anyone else, all the better. In this instance, as in most, customers (realtors in this example), want to stay in their environment or own website and not have to leave to navigate another site.

None of these are difficult. They are relatively simple additions but makes engagement simpler, faster and would result in less hassle.

PayIt

Do monopolies have any incentive to lower the hassle for their customers? No, not really. Yes, they may tire of complaints and may employ technology to help them be more efficient and that technology may somehow help customers be efficient too, but it likely wouldn't be designed with the intent of pure efficiency on the customer.

A category of a monopoly is governments and government agencies. There are lots of them. According to Michael

Plunkett, the co-founder of PayIt, there are roughly 80,000 state, county and city local governments and agencies in the U.S. Each have specific functions and we citizens must engage many of them to pay taxes, to get licenses, permits, and to register for various activities like voting.

PayIt is a company devoted to making engagement with governments and agencies friendlier and easier. All I need to mention is the acronym DMV, and most of you know what I mean if you aren't shuddering already. Any and every time you engage a government or agency, it is going to be time-consuming, and costly. The DMV is a great example that most everyone reading this has had to endure.

It's a monumental undertaking for PayIt but fortunately, part of their solution involves helping government and associated agencies with back-office efficiencies. I believe there are likely ample opportunities to help make our governments and agencies become more efficient using technology.

From a citizen perspective, imagine such things as your registration and insurance certificates on a mobile app so that if, and when, you get pulled over you aren't sorting through your over-stuffed glove compartment looking for them only to find that your insurance certificate is from the old policy. Imagine when you must register your new vehicle and having all the forms you need, completing applications all in the palm of your hand.

There are so many possibilities. What if you could pay a traffic or parking fine online and in an efficient manner. What if you wanted to find out your polling location? What if you wanted to apply for a hunting license and receive it without traveling to the fish and game commission office? What if you were having your house remodeled and you needed a building permit and could do that with a mobile app in under a minute?

What if you were notified via text that your personal property taxes were due in 30 days and provided a link to accomplish that? The possibilities are endless, and I think very exciting.

PayIt is a company founded on the premise that they are going to improve the *Hassle Quotient* for citizens. They know there is no incentive for any government or agency to do it. They have no competition and it's up to us citizens to abide by laws and regulations no matter how painful. They plan to reduce the amount of time it takes to engage any government. They want to reduce the effort by giving us mobile applications to have immediate access to documents, they want to reduce the costs of engagement and make the experience of working with governments and agencies on par with dealing with commercial enterprises.

PayIt estimates that $2 trillion exchanges between citizens and governments and that doesn't include what is transacted with the Federal Government. It is possible, but this will take some time, but I love that their entire business is built on lowering the Hassle Quotient for citizens. I am a big fan and hoping they succeed in a big way.

Nebraska Furniture Mart

This Omaha-based home furnishing company started in 1937 in the basement of a shop in Omaha, Nebraska. Today, with four stores (Omaha, Des Moines, Kansas City and Dallas), it boasts the largest single store offering home furnishings, floorings, appliances and electronics. It's newest store, in Dallas, TX has over 560,000 square feet of retail space with a distribution center spanning the space of over 20 football fields.

Nebraska Furniture Mart stocks over 40,000 items and has available over 260,000 items online. In 1983, the founder, Rose Blumkin sold 90% of her interest in the business to Berkshire Hathaway for $55 million. While the company is rolled up into Berkshire Hathaway, the two stores in Omaha and Kansas City each average more than $500 million in sales annually. Those two stores combined deliver more than 1,000 orders each day and deliver to 2500 cities in 5 states. Nebraska Furniture Mart has become the largest home furnishing's company in the United States and largely because of its culture and adoption of the *Hassle Quotient.*

In Kansas City, I only know of one furniture store that survived the dominance of Nebraska Furniture Mart. NFM has always offered low pricing. Rose Blumkin made sure and at one time sold merchandise for 5% above cost to capture market share. Today, NFM merchandisers spent much of their time scanning the web to ensure NFM is offering the lowest price.

They excel at the customer experience. Their stores are fresh, modern and well decorated. Their furniture is displayed as if in a home. They have ample sales people walking the store floor, each carrying a tablet that provides inventory levels and the ability to complete a transaction without having to go through a check-out line. Once, knowing exactly what I wanted, I was in and out of their store within 15 minutes having purchased a new OLED television set and went through their drive-in merchandise pick up and hauled it home.

NFM is a master of offering interest-free financing for at least 6 months and many times offers free delivery. I have a lake house in central Missouri and they service that area with 7-8 trucks every weekend. Recently, they delivered a new patio set that we bought online from their Omaha location and it was delivered by 8:00 AM. I asked the driver if they had stayed at a hotel and his answer was no. They left Kansas City at 5AM and had a full truck with 12 stops to deliver at the lake.

They have a wide variety of merchandise and a comprehensive website with a robust search engine. My personal experience is I can find what I am looking for so long as it is home furnishings, flooring, electronics or appliances. I have the option of picking it up immediately or waiting a day or two to have it delivered. Their pricing is as good or better than other options and the overall experience is extremely good. I cannot think of anything they can do to improve upon the experience. Yes, the stores are large, and it might take extra time to find what you are shopping for, but it's the nature of their product that causes that. I don't have to visit the store. I could shop online but if I want to really see the quality of the merchandise, color or other attributes, I have that option.

Nebraska Furniture Mart is a dominant company in the markets they serve and a great example of how an enterprising lady with strong beliefs led a culture that led to Warren Buffet investing and taking the business to the next level.

WeFixFreight

Yes, the name of this company is perhaps confusing to those not in the industry, but it denotes exactly what they do. Many may not know this, but the lion's share of shipping in the U.S., is done using full truckload services. Less than 5% of the time, it's possible that a truckload of palletized product might shift in-transit and even fall over in the truck due to perhaps taking a corner too fast or coming to a stop too fast. Customers receiving these types of loads expect the contents of truckloads to have intact, shrink-wrapped pallets that are easy to offload using a forklift. In fact, if a trucker attempts to deliver a load where even one or a few pallets have shifted, they could refuse the entire load, or refuse the pallets that have shifted.

When that happens, the trucker must find a resource to correct the problem, usually a facility with a dock and crew that can unload the shifted pallets and re-stack and re-shrink wrap them. Given that truckers are typically nowhere near their own facilities, they must find a source that can accommodate and fix these loads, not an easy task. It takes many phone calls, finding a facility that is dock high, with a staff willing to fix the load and get them on their way. There is also the complication of negotiating a price to fix this. Like many businesses, when a vendor knows a customer is in dire need, the price can fluctuate and, in this case, be unreasonable.

Yes, this is quite the niche business, but WeFixFreight saw this as an opportunity to provide a solution that requires less time and effort for a trucker, sets a national price in advance and applies technology, including a mobile application to make the user experience better than the alternative. Yes, they have used the *Hassle Quotient* and are now rapidly growing. Trucklers and freight brokers only need to access the WeFixFreight website or mobile application, complete essential information and are directed to one of over 150 facilities contracted nationwide. They have established a large network to minimize miles a trucker has to drive to have his load fixed.

All parties know in advance the exact cost so there no leverage due to extenuating circumstances. WeFixFreight also arranges to provide storage for refused loads or pallets so the trucker can go on to their next job while disposition is being determined. They also can send crews to highway scales to fix overloads and deliver freight if a trucker needs that type of assistance.

WeFixFreight is a niche business but found that truckers and freight brokers were spending too much time and effort to find a solution when a load shifted. They also knew that truckers and freight brokers could be "held hostage" with unreasonable fees and thus set up their network with prenegotiated rates. And by enabling engagement via their website or mobile app, made the user experience much better than making a series of phone calls trying to find someone who could help.

I used the primary examples of Amazon, Uber and Netflix as companies who have adopted the *Hassle Quotient*, knowingly or not, to become a dominant company in their market space. However, as pointed out here, you don't have to be a mega-company to be successful using the *Hassle Quotient*. Yes, that might be the outcome if you make it easier for your customers to engage you by requiring less of their time, make it easy for them, provide a competitive price and the very best user experience available.

But does all this work if you are a product-based company? All the examples used so far are about service companies. In the next chapter we will explore how product-based companies can leverage the same formula to achieve market dominance.

Chapter 10 – Durable Goods Companies and the Hassle Quotient

Every company provides a service, though not every company is a service company. The *Hassle Quotient* applies to all companies except perhaps monopolies. They don't have a real incentive to deliver the lowest possible *Hassle Quotient* and many times monopolies are regulated, as they have no competition. Thus, a regulatory body needs to control the components of the *Hassle Quotient* formula, especially pricing and even service quality at times.

I love the show Shark Tank. I think I like it because I have sought venture capital funding a couple times. It wasn't on a television show, but the questions are all the same. It's amazing to me how many people are so unprepared and don't realize how important sales traction counts toward valuation and ultimately getting a deal. I especially find it interesting that at least 90% of those making a pitch have a company centered around a product. Service-centered companies don't make the cut near as much as those who have invented a product or modified a product. Maybe it's because you are more likely to get a patent on a product than a process.

Mark Cuban is famous for saying "You don't have a company, you have a product." Essentially, he is saying that when you have a company, come back and I might be interested. Or, if the Sharks like a product but don't have a viable company established or being possible, they offer a licensing deal. One of the key things the Sharks look for is expansion beyond the original product. What else can be developed that are extensions of the product that can extend their business. Pet rocks were once a huge fad, but fads have short life cycles and it died out and there wasn't another product to supplement or replace it. That's in contrast to the iPhone which has developed multiple generations, each with new features and improvements, but Apple has launched the iPad, iPod, iWatch, iTunes and more. That makes for a company.

The other show I like a lot is the Profit. That show typically centers on family run small businesses that might be service-oriented or product oriented. Marcus does a great job deploying the elements of the *Hassle Quotient*, looking to improve the customer experience, reduce the amount of time and effort it takes a customer to engage, and making the price competitive though he often makes the trade-off that many good and great companies make, trading lowest price for best experience. He summarizes his *Hassle Quotient* as People, Process and Product.

As you might suspect, I believe service-oriented companies are prime candidates to adopt the *Hassle Quotient* and constantly work to improve the factors especially in contrast to their competitors. But the *Hassle Quotient* isn't relegated solely for service companies. It applies to product companies. No matter what kind of company one operates there is a service element to it and a dominant company ensures that they are the best when requiring time and effort from customers, price competitively and provide the very best service in advance of the sale and more importantly, the post-sale experience.

I mentioned Apple, so let's dig deeper into their *Hassle Quotient*. Their products are amazing and all about saving people time, effort and with mostly a great user experience. The iPhone is so much more than a phone, it's a very powerful hand-held computer, and more powerful than those early day computers that would fill an entire room.

I joke that I used to own a GPS device. What a great invention. Way back in the day, I'm old enough to have used maps. Yes, the kind that fold out but for mw, almost impossible to fold back. Or, the book that contained maps where states like Pennsylvania required two pages. Transitioning from one page to another was always a bit of a challenge. Then with the internet and before GPS became commonplace, you could get directions online and print those. But when I got my first GPS I thought it was great, giving me turn by turn directions and warning me in advance when I had to navigate a turn. I was never nervous about traveling after that.

But the GPS device was short-lived and was replaced by a mobile app that could be downloaded onto a smart phone. A very cool device was replaced by a mobile app on the smartphone because it cost less, took less time and effort, and ultimately became a better experience. I remember having to download updated maps and routes on my stand-alone GPS device and I think the update alone cost me $50. Now, with an app, any changes are updated without my knowledge, and at no cost. The user experience also has improved because now, in addition to basic directions, I now am guided based on traffic congestion. I might not be routed the shortest route but am routed the quickest. How great is that?

At one time I had an iPod to play all my music. I downloaded the songs I wanted from my PC and various CDs and had the ability to plug directly in to my vehicle, so I can listen while driving. That didn't last long as my smartphone now contains a music library and can download new tunes anytime I want. No need to carry around an additional piece of hardware when I can use my smartphone. In fact, Apple recently announced they are discontinuing most versions of the iPod, including the Nano and the mini.

And way back when, I once had a digital camera. Oh, what an improvement over the conventional cameras that I had to load film, remove and take to a drug store or mail off to develop prints. Amazing technology advancement and followed the principles of the *Hassle Quotient*. Took less time, a lot less effort, cost was lower when counting development costs and the experience was superior. But, as we all know, my digital camera now is part of my smart device. Very convenient and I use it far more now than when I had a separate digital camera device.

I'm going to date myself, but I remember when the microwave was the new item. It saved people time and effort to warm food and provide a superior user experience to warming up the oven or heating something on the stove top. I remember when the self-propelled mower came out. Talk about something that saved a ton of effort! It also saved a lot time. When the calculator was invented and replaced the slide rule, that was like a miracle from heaven. Now there's an app for that. Think about all the products you have recently purchased. Maybe you bought something to replace an item that wore out or broke, but if you bought a new device, I'll bet it had features to save time, save effort or provide a superior user experience.

More evidence? One of the hottest gadgets out there are the home devices that you speak instructions to. I have the Echo. It saves me time from having to pick up a device and push my finger to launch an application and find a song I want played or find out the weather conditions. Yes, that's how lazy I have become. "Siri, what was the score of the game last night?" I'm too lazy to open an app! You see what our behavior is? We want it fast, simple and convenient.

Those are examples of how products can meet the elements of the *Hassle Quotient*. Create a product that saves customers time, saves them effort, costs less than the alternative and provide a superior experience to the alternative and you likely have a winner. However, products can be easily duplicated, and the next manufacturer figures out how to create one extra feature or take a little bit of cost out, and now your product lags the market. If you have a winner, one that dominates, how long do you think it is before you have a handful of competitors with a better product?

Regardless of that rat race, a company that makes a product must provide a great service before the sale, and support after the sale, if they have any hope of being a dominant company. In today's world, whether you sell a service or a product, you better have a website. If you don't, put this book down and immediately go hire someone to put one out there for you. It's absolutely a must. However, not every company with a website is an e-commerce site, or one where a consumer or customer can purchase their items. That is okay. For example, you might run a high-end jewelry store and you want to use a website to promote yourself, but it might be more important for a customer to see your goods in person.

If you have a physical store, let's talk about how to meet the components of the *Hassle Quotient*. If you want to save your customers time, remember the old saying: location, location, location. They are going to drive to you so make sure you are in a convenient part of town with great access and ample parking. You want them to exert less effort, greet them or have someone greet them as they come in. I recall a retailer who had staff greet customers at the door with a "welcome back". If the customer stated they hadn't been there before, it was an opportunity to welcome them and personally offer to assist them with anything they needed. Great touch. Otherwise, use the opportunity to help them find what they came for. This is especially true for big box retailers.

There isn't anything worse, for this male who hates to shop, to have to wander around the store just trying to find what I am seeking. The faster I can find it, the faster I can decide to buy it. Yes, I might see something else that tempts me, but I came to that store for a purpose and I don't want to shop and see what might be new. This probably goes without saying, but for Pete's sake have sufficient staff at check out. I detest seeing 20 check-out lanes that are staffed by 3 cashiers. That typically means I am going to wait in line and frustrate me. Yes, Walmart I am speaking to you. Don't laugh grocery store, you are on my list as well. You should make it a habit of studying when you are busy and when you aren't. I know it is cyclical and predictable and you might gain customers if you can have them spend less time than they do at their competitors.

While I'm at it. Why not have valet service? I see valet service all the time at nice restaurants and rarely am I hauling large bags or boxes out of a restaurant. Save me time and I will reward you with loyalty. Save me effort and you are golden. Yes, I might pay more, but that only makes you a good or great company and not a dominant one. So, save me time, save me effort and save me money.

Another important one is the overall experience you put me through. Experience means a lot of things and we have covered the amount of time you require of me and the effort I must exert. For a retail store, I want an experience with a clean, well-lit store that is highly organized with wide aisles and mostly with friendly customer-focused staff. Their number one job priority should be to satisfy me and when they have time, can stock shelves, or better do that at night.

In the Kansas City area, there are a good number of Quick Trip convenience stores. What I like best about them is they have ample fuel pumps, it is well lit, they have multiple cashiers with little wait and they take the time to regularly power-wash the concrete near the gas pumps. When someone spills gas by overflowing their tank, especially if its diesel fuel, that can cause quite a stain and even odor. Most convenience stores or gas stations don't pay attention to that. Quick Trip goes the extra length and ensures their concrete is clean, their trash cans not full and plenty of windshield washer with ample paper cloths. Their gas prices are competitive, and you can buy a 32oz. fountain drink for $.99. Yes, they dominate the KC market for convenience stores.

For those of you who have websites, and especially for those of you selling items, your job is very difficult. After all, unless you are selling something extremely unique or proprietary, Amazon might be your competition. I can't tell you how important it is to have someone engineer your site so that the average person can understand what it is you do or sell and that better happen within 4 seconds. Remember one of our core behavioral traits? We are all impatient and will move on very quickly.

Secondly, I want as few pages as possible to navigate your site. I need a robust search engine to find what I am looking for. I want to see how others have rated your product and or service. I want to see what questions they have. I need to know what shipping will cost, if not free, and I want to know that without clicking six different pages or icons. If you are selling clothing items, provide a sizing chart that is relevant and again without having to click 6 times and figure out how to get back to where I was.

Checkout is very important. Unless you like abandoned shopping carts, you need to provide an easy process with as few page changes as possible. You should allow your customer to check out as a guest and if they elect they will sign up as they might return and want to save time by having them save their name, shipping address, credit card information and the like. Ask me if it's okay to send them promotional emails and they will let you know. Don't just assume that they want it and spam them. Give them an accurate estimate of delivery date and keep them updated on their order whereabouts as it is shipped.

If you don't know exactly how to do all this, buy something on Amazon and take notes on the number of pages they put your through and the time it takes to process an order. They do it well. Copy the best processes you can find. If you are a business owner, you are also a consumer. Pay attention to what you like and copy that process.

Have a modern look on your website. Yes, it costs a little bit of money, but your website says a lot about your brand and how much you care.

The trend of videos becoming more important in the makeup of a website is real. It is believed that viewers are 7 times for likely to purchase or engage themselves with a website that has a video on its landing page. Remember, people are naturally lazy, and you make a web visitor's life easier by telling them a story via video than you can be writing and including a lot of text in your website.

Software

Without a doubt software meets many of the *Hassle Quotient* criteria. Microsoft was as close to a dominant company as there was. They had products that saved people time, required little effort to be exerted, price was, while not low, a bargain compared to what efficiency they could deliver compared to the alternative method, and by their very nature, provided a good customer experience. Some would dispute that as there is a huge support component to the customer experience and they are so large, they cannot or don't provide a personal touch when dealing with issues.

However, they have many licensed service providers that can, and do, provide support on behalf of Microsoft. However, since Microsoft was dominant, they attracted competition and quite a lot of competition. While many tried, Apple and Google have been the companies to succeed in taking them from their dominant position. Maybe they got comfortable with their position. I don't know, but I have worked for a lot of companies that have had success, lost their edge, fear of change set in and sat on their laurels. They quit talking to their customers to learn the customer's impression and the next thing they knew, someone came in and transforms their industry.

I believe that software companies constantly must be modifying, upgrading and transforming their work. I've said before that every keystroke counts. Software engineers need to not only develop code but develop the process so that the customer understands fully how to operate it and use all its functionality. It must be intuitive in today's world. Gone are the days where a software company can develop code that radically improves some process and makes it more efficient yet requires deep and costly training. The key is to develop code and a user interface so intuitive that a teenager can understand it, operate it and teach others to do that. Otherwise, competitors are lurking everywhere and will take the next step and take you from a great company to a good company or even worse.

Unless you manufacture something and have responsibility for its overall design and functionality, you are a service company. If you are a retailer, you are a service company. You just happen to sell certain products, but it's all about the amount of time and effort you put your customers through to engage you, about your price points compared to other competitive retailers and very much about the overall experience you provide your customer. How well lit and organized is your store? How engaging is your staff? How easy is it to buy something? How clean is your store? What are your return policies and practices? What else do you do that says you take the extra step?

If you manufacture something, you are providing a service when you sell your product, train consumers how to use it, provide support, take returns and provide a warranty. However, if you manufacture something, you have competitors that manufacture the same thing, or something very similar. Your product must consider the components of the Hassle Quotient to become a dominant company. Your product needs to save people time. Your product must save effort. Your product must be priced competitively, or lower than others, and you must provide an exceptional experience, just like a retailer, even though you might be a wholesaler.

Many companies think that if they sell a product cheaper, that is the secret to success. It's not. If you don't provide the same user experience, save consumer's time and effort, someone will come along and out-price them and it becomes a vicious cycle.

Yes, durable goods-based companies have every reason to follow and adopt the *Hassle Quotient* as do service-oriented companies. In fact, durable goods-based companies have service components about them that can differentiate themselves from their competitors. If you think about new products that are introduced, they have at least one element of the Hassle Quotient as their calling card.

"Our product saves you time!" "Our new widget makes your life easier." "The new bullet widget only costs $9.99." "When you buy the acme life is better product, your life will improve." Everyone single product introduced has at least one of the features of the Hassle Quotient. Every single one. The more they have, the better. However, in the product world, new products become targets for competitors to knock off by being easier, simpler, less costly or provide a better experience.

Chapter 11 - It's the Small Things that Count

I like a bargain. I really do. I mean, who doesn't? Billionaires like bargains. I like bargains and we all like bargains. However, for many of us, we must weigh the monetary price of the bargain compared to the pain of the process. We must weigh how much time, how much effort and what the experience is going to be to get that bargain.

Here is a great example, it's called the rebate. Typically, rebates are far better deals than a small percentage off the product. However, you must jump through a lot of hoops to file rebates. It is not uncommon to have to send in the original receipt and even remove bar codes from the original packaging in your own envelope and paying for postage. According to the Wall Street Journal, 40% of rebates are not redeemed or filed improperly even though the product was likely purchased due to the value of the rebate.

It's a great example of going through a lot of effort and time to get the bargain you want. In my opinion, it's too much pain unless the rebate is more than $100.

You want a bargain in purchasing groceries? Aldi might just fit the bill. However, they have limited selections especially in the produce and meats section. Their stores are about a quarter the size of a standard grocery store, yet they have a section in the store devoted to durable consumer goods, whose selection of items change all the time. It's like some buyer at Aldi finds great deals for some household items and the price is just too good to pass up. They find rock bottom deals and then place them in the middle of the store for no rhyme nor reason especially because when a certain item is sold out, it likely won't be stocked again. They do this and use their space in this method instead of having a larger fresh produce or meat section. I suppose it works for them!

What I am sure of is Aldi goes out of its way to illustrate and demonstrate they are a discount grocery chain. They decided that it costs too much money to have an employee regularly collect shopping carts from the parking lot, so they charge a $.25 deposit to use a cart and you get that back when you return it to the rack adjacent to the store. Another sign is they do not provide free bags. A shopper needs to bring their own bags or just not use bags and take home your items loosely. There are no fancy displays and racking is minimal. Aldi prefers to simply stack boxes of product to offer their product. If you haven't visited an Aldi, I would suggest that after a single visit you would deduce that they use lots of tactics to reduce costs and "pass the savings to the consumer."

Here is another example. Costco is a wholesale club. Their model is that of a membership model whereby your annual subscription helps offset the cost of goods, so you can buy things cheaper. And, they play the packaging game two ways. First, and most famously, they can share savings because the items they save use less packaging than conventional grocery stores. Basically, you buy in bulk and that saves you money because you buy larger quantities and they don't have to use smaller packaging. Want a box of Nabisco Wheat Thins? It's a big box, twice the size of normal, and it contains two bags of Thins inside. They save a penny on the exterior packaging and pass the savings on to the consumer.

And, like Aldi, they don't provide shopping bags when you check out. You bring your own, or more ingeniously, they supply you with the cardboard boxes that their stock arrives in. Rather than spend a lot of money trashing or recycling their cardboard out the back door, they let the consumers use the cardboard to carry their goods home and then dispose or recycle from home. Boom! Consumers become personal waste management resources. They save money and give the shopper a better experience. Why doesn't Aldi do that? It saves me from carrying out 10 cans of peas in my arms to the car! You see, it's the little things. By the way, Costco does have free use of carts and uses employees to haul the carts back to the store. Maybe that's what the annual membership fee is for.

My point is that it can be a compilation of little things that can make a big difference with the amount of time required for a consumer to engage a company, the amount of effort you require, and the overall customer experience. And, the dominant companies are constantly investing in technology to improve efficiencies that lower costs that are passed on to their customers. Little things add up and little things count a lot.

I don't want to give the impression that only large, internet-centric companies can dominate. That isn't the case at all. Local companies can dominate, but those that have been in existence for any time, likely are a trade-off company. They are likely competing on price but making customers suffer through additional time, effort or a less-than-desirable experience.

To be clear, it's hard to dominate. Very hard. How does one who provides the best overall experience also be a price leader? How do they pay for that experience? That is absolutely where the rubber hits the proverbial road. That is where technology often comes to play. To be a price leader, a company likely must uber-efficient and extremely cost-effective. They might have to settle for lower margins too.

When you are a dominant company, you can save in marketing. You don't have to exclaim; "Hey, look at us, we are a dominant company…come buy from us." Your zealous customers and disciples will do that for you. You will save money by not having to spend a lot of money to increase your exposure and tell people how much time, effort and money you will save them and then provide the best experience possible.

Small local companies can dominate. They can provide a service or a product that makes them stand out from their competitors because they provide a superior customer experience that requires less time and effort than their competitors and at a price that is competitive or lower than other options.

If you operate a pizza parlor in Peoria, you can dominate by being the best pizza parlor in Peoria. You do that by providing your customers the most convenient location, deliver their food the fastest and highly competitive prices and with a great experience inside your parlor and great-tasting pizza, or at least better than all other pizza in Peoria.

Time and Effort

A good starting point for any company is to ask your customers and listen to them about how your company compares on the components of the Hassle Quotient. Ask them for suggestions and ideas. They are your very best source of ideas and can give them what they want. Reverse engineer it. Start with the customer experience and work backward. It's not about you. It's about them.

If you operate a service business, find a way to respond more quickly. Nothing worse than a plumber who can't respond and service a customer for a week. That is too much time and a terrible experience. Maybe you need to partner and give up some profit but find a way to respond more quickly. If you do, you will be remembered, and loyalty ensues.

Here is a little thing that to some might be a big thing. I frequent Great Clips to get my hair cut every month or so. I used to go to a fancy and expensive salon but the cost and especially the rigor of calling in and figuring out an appointment that worked for me and the stylist just became a big hassle. So, one day, when I needed a cut and didn't have time to make an appointment with my stylist, I walked into the local Great Clips.

I knew it would save me a lot of money but wasn't confident I would get a quality cut. When I walked in the store, their stylists were all busy and on the counter was a monitor with a list of clients in order of priority. I was manually added to the list which was about 6 people long. As I was waiting, a gentleman walked in and within a minute was seated and getting his hair cut. I immediately thought that there must be a mistake because I had been there for nearly 10 minutes and he just got there.

When my turn came I asked my stylist about it and was informed that if I were to use their mobile app, I could check in from my house and when I did that would be advised how long the current wait time was and that I would take priority over walk-in traffic. Sold! I downloaded the app and ever since have checked in online to minimize my wait time. Yes, I got an excellent cut and it was priced about half of my salon. It was the Hassle Quotient unfolding before my eyes before I had even hypothesized on it. Just the simple ability to check in online without being there sold me and now I am a loyal customer. Save me time and you likely will have my patronage.

Customer Experience

Here's a customer experience that is small but so impactful. My friend is a greeter at his church on Sundays. It's a fairly large church, or one large enough where not everyone knows everyone and one where it is very common to have visitors every Sunday. As you might expect, a greeter's job is to make both members and visitors feel welcome and at ease. It is important to make the right first impression and that is exactly the role of the greeter.

Without being told, my friend decided that rather than lead with a handshake to welcome the adults, when a family came to the front door, he would pick out the kids and get down low and offer a fist bump. Yes, a fist bump. Now how unconventional is that for a church and cool for a kid to get recognized before the parents with a fist bump. You know who enjoys the fist bump more than anyone? The parents. That is a perfect example of a little thing that makes a huge impact in the experience.

I learned a long time ago that people like to do business with people they like. It's a natural human behavior. Have you ever gone into a business where someone knows your name and greets you that way? Do you know how that makes you feel? I don't know about you, but it makes me feel special. For someone to remember my name and care enough, it's a very comforting. If you run a small business, see if you can't remember the names and personally get to know your customers. If you are terrible at remembering names, like me, hire someone who is great at that. It will enhance the customer experience you provide tenfold.

Lots of things go into customer experience. If you operate a store, keep it clean. Make sure it is well lit. Make sure you have easy navigation, so customers can find what they are seeking faster. Greet them as they come in. Train your staff to devote themselves to helping customers first and stocking or whatever they do secondary. These small things matter.

Make sure you have a website. Make sure it is modern and has easy navigation. Yes, a decent website might cost two or three times what a cheap one would cost, but you want a website that your customers want to experience. It's not about you. It's about them.

Absolutely, positively have sufficient checkout staff doing just that, checking customers out. People hate waiting in line like they hate waiting in traffic. If you operate a larger company, capture data that can be analyzed to figure out what customers are buying and when they are buying. Make it easier for them to buy what they want and easy to check out. Don't put the most popular items in the back of the store just so they will pass your other items and maybe buy one of those.

Make your return policy simple and hassle-free. Yes, you can put guidelines around returns. Just make certain your customers know them, so they don't get the unpleasant surprise when they need to use it.

If you offer a service business, offer guarantees. You can guarantee satisfaction, or you can guarantee response times. Guarantees work! Guarantees are a better customer experience than using a service that won't stand behind their work or commit to serving a customer in a short period of time. I've always said that if I wanted something tomorrow, I would ask for it tomorrow. That is another way of saying I am impatient and like most of you, I want it now.

If you are a service company and have a wide customer audience, maybe a mobile app would make a better experience or save your customer time and effort. Remember, texting is more popular than calling someone on the phone. It's our nature. We would rather engage, in today's world, electronically than to have to go through a phone call.

And for goodness sake, answer your phone and with a human. Every interaction is a chance to shine and sell something. I detest calling any of the credit card companies I use. How many options do I have to select to actually talk to someone? I've had experience where I press zero hoping to talk to someone and get a recorded menu. It's a terrible experience. I'm sure it saves them a lot of money but costs them a lot of customers.

I once worked for a company where we were not allowed to screen calls. I didn't have an assistant to take my calls. I did. Yes, we prefer to engage electronically when we can but there are times where we want and need to speak to someone so accommodate those who want to do that. It's a better experience and saves the customer a lot of time.

Use straightforward, open and simple pricing formats. Don't make a customer think they didn't or forgot to read the fine print. I can't think of a worse pricing strategy than LTL carriers as I pointed out earlier. They state pricing as a percentage discount off some obscure and complicated tariff. I don't care that I get an 80% discount. 80% off what? What is the bottom line?

I guess it's better than most healthcare where you only find out the costs when you get your bill. They don't make it easy for consumers to "shop" the market. That is a terrible experience. And prescription drug pricing can be incredibly difficult to understand with various insurance programs, generic drugs and the like. I recently went to my drug store to pick up a prescription that was issued after a doctor visit. When they were ringing it up and I saw the price, I politely declined and walked out. I had to call my doctor and ask for an alternative which was 1/20th of the cost of the original prescription. A waste of time, effort and terrible experience.

Recently on NBC nightly news, they reported that it can often be more advantageous for consumers to ask their pharmacist for the "cash price." For some reason, pharmacists are not allowed to inform anyone of the cash price without the consumer asking. Say what? It's no wonder our healthcare is so broken and subject for another book by a more informed author.

I like to know what I am spending before I commit. I wouldn't think of paying a painter by the hour without knowing the number of hours. Bad experience. For technicians who like to charge by the hour, think about increasing the amount of flat rate charges you use. After all, you are the professional and should know what the job at hand takes, unless, of course, you haven't performed that job before.

As I stated earlier, it's likely easier to start a business and adopt the culture that supports the covenants of the *Hassle Quotient*. Existing businesses really struggle with change, especially if they think they are doing well. They don't suspect that their competitors or start-ups are constantly thinking of ways to knock them off. It doesn't necessarily take a complete overhaul to start the process to adopt the *Hassle Quotient*. It's a summation of many things and often very small things that can make the difference of being a good or great company, to one that can dominate.

Chapter 12 - Summary

Regardless of whether dominant companies like Amazon, Uber, Netflix, Nebraska Furniture Mart or Quick Trip realize it, they have followed and continue to do so to get to be in the dominant position they are in their respective markets.

$$Hassle\ Quotient = \frac{Time + Effort + Cost}{User\ Experience}$$

Their objective has been to lower the hassle of the customer by minimizing the amount of time and effort required for customers to engage them, offer lower prices than competitors and providing the very best possible user experience. They do not trade-off one component of the formula for another. They deliver on all elements. They ask their customers how they are doing, and they constantly invest in methods and technology to constantly improve.

You don't have to have a company that saves your customer time, effort and money while giving them a superior experience over an alternative or over your competitor. You can go the old route and pick one discipline, focus on that and excel at it. You can decide that you are going to sell your product or service at a lower price point than anyone else and hope that the competition doesn't find a way to beat your price. Hope isn't a strategy. You might end up having a nice company, maybe even a good one. Who knows, if all the stars align maybe you grow it into a great company.

However, in today's world, if you don't excel at everything all at the same time, you will never be a dominant company. It's too easy, especially in today's world, for someone to come along and bump you off the perch you selected to take your stand.

Remember the Netflix story and how they got started? They beat Blockbuster on the amount of effort it took for a consumer to engage them. They made sure their price point was lower with a subscription model than the transactional model for their average consumer, and then made the overall experience, especially the video return experience, superior by not requiring the consumer to drive anywhere to return their DVD. Consumers only had to place the DVD in the return postage-paid envelope and drop in their mail box. Not much easier than that. However, they didn't answer the "save the customer time" element. With Blockbuster, a consumer, at the last minute, could decide "tonight is movie night" and drive to their local Blockbuster store, find something worth watching (maybe not what they set out to watch given the inventory limitation of Blockbuster), and return home and watch immediately. With Netflix, you had to wait at least one day. Netflix didn't check all the boxes to dominate.

Maybe they knew it, maybe they didn't, but Netflix would have been a prime target for someone to transform and bring video streaming to the market so that one could instantaneously download the movie of their choice. Right now. Without getting in the car and driving down the road. Right now.

Netflix didn't wait for someone else to transform the industry. They transformed themselves, brought streaming to the mix and ended the mail option. In fact, here, just a few short years into streaming of Netflix, it's almost humorous to think that DVDs used to be mailed! What? Why not send it by carrier pigeon or have a Fred Flintstone or Barney Rubble deliver it on a dinosaur. We know what happened, and they became, and still are, a dominant company, even though Amazon, yes Amazon, has a competing offering.

One of the most important things to take away from this book is that you don't have to create an Amazon, Uber or Netflix to dominate. This formula works for small or local businesses. If you are an entrepreneur, or a want-to-be entrepreneur, you can have a dominant company, even if it is in your local neighborhood. You must save your customers more time, effort and money than their alternative and provide them the best experience they can get. Yes, it's hard. If it was easy, everyone would be doing it....right? You must work hard to save your customers time, effort and money all while delivering the best customer experience. You cannot rest. You cannot think you have accomplished all that and sit back. You can't because competitors are always going to be nipping at your heels to try and save a customer just a little bit more time, or a little bit more effort than you do. Maybe they will figure out how to lower costs while giving a similar experience that you do. Do not rest. Continue talking and learning from your customers. Find out what is most important to them and how you compare to your competitors.

If you own an existing business, the very best thing you can do is to ask your current customers their opinions and how you compare. Ask them for ideas on how you can save them time. Ask them about the amount of effort they exert with the alternative option or competitor. Ask them how your prices compare. And go in depth to ask about their total experience with you compared to others. Ask them what they like. Ask them what they don't like and ask for ideas. Your best advice comes from your current customers and not from you.

If you own a business, start thinking about your customer the first thing in the morning, the middle of the day and at the end of it. Dream about your customer and if your business is keeping you awake, make sure it is your customer doing it and nothing else. Being efficient is good, but only if it translates directly to the customer benefit. Making money is good and even critical, but only if it is because you realize it's because of your customers.

Let me give you an example. American Airlines has been in business since 1930 and a very important revenue stream is for the cargo they move in the belly of their aircraft, at least when there aren't so many suitcases that cargo can still fit. Actually, by charging for baggage, it's a form of air cargo.

Anyway, at a conference a few years ago, I met their new Director of Strategy. She was a very intelligent and articulate woman and I had to ask about the airline's strategy with cargo. I was most curious as to why it wasn't evident that a consumer could ship cargo with American. I knew that American, like most airlines, catered to freight forwarders who secured shippers and cargo and then arranged first and final mile while airlines like American handled the linehaul or airline leg component. In essence, American Airlines is like a wholesaler making its belly capacity available to forwarders.

I suggested that they could be a dominant air cargo provider had they opted to service the direct business shipper and consumer. They could offer the first, middle and final mile and cut-out the middle man. After all, they supplied the most critical factor, the linehaul capacity. Ultimately, she wasn't sure, but suggested it was that way, because it had always been that way. By offering a direct cargo service, they could cut the middle man out, likely save shippers time, money, effort and provide a better overall experience. George Bernard Shaw said "Don't see things as they are and ask why. See things as they can be and ask why not. John F Kennedy used a similar quote, but it's great advice for anyone in a company.

Same thing applies in the LTL industry. Certain things have been that way since 1935. Now, the third-party logistics industry is going to be a $1.1 trillion industry by 2024 and LTL carriers will continue to transition to wholesaler model.

For American, it would be a significant change to their business model. It's not always a wholesale change to become a dominant company. Sometimes, it's only one or two things. Here is an example: My friend operates a local courier company. I asked if I wanted to move something across town, could I download his app, insert my payment information and order service? His answer was no, I would have to call and set up an account. Really? Don't you want to appeal to the mass market? People don't want to make that effort and call someone. They want to download, upload and go. Now there are startups that simply bring the experience of the mobile app to the forefront and not have the experience of a professional providing the service.

One of the biggest benefits of becoming a dominant company, or practicing elements of the Hassle Quotient, is the viral marketing that will result. We live in a connected world. I can find a review, or more important, someone's opinion on about anything by searching the internet. More importantly, when people visit, they like to share both good stories and bad. You don't hear many conversations that relate to someone's mediocre experience with a company. It's either an outrageously horrific story or where someone had a really good experience. I know you want to be part of the latter.

But viral marketing saves from having to spend huge dollars on conventional marketing schemes. Those dollars can translate back to your bottom line, and of course, to lowering your prices if you need to.

Just about once per week, there has been a story about Amazon. For example, this week, they announced they will start delivering groceries from Whole Foods within a two-hour window in select markets. Sound familiar? Who is the beneficiary of that strategy? Why? If you don't know by now, you might want to go back to Chapter 1 and re-read this book. In the case of Amazon, with every announcement they make, or you hear, think about how it impacts the Hassle Quotient. I believe you will start looking at them in a different light. Hopefully, you will start thinking of all companies, including yours, on how they are adopting the

Hassle Quotient to start down the path of being a dominant company.

I hope you have taken a small nugget from this book that you can use to improve the company for which you work. Everyone wants to work for a good or great company. Might even be better to work for a dominant company. I believe there is a common thread and I call it the Hassle Quotient. Dominant companies go to the extreme to make it easy for customers to engage them. It's harder than it sounds. It's especially hard if you work for a company that has been around for a while as it takes a cultural change. So many companies operate to deliver financial results. They talk about putting the customer first but don't put it into practice. By taking a few nuggets from this book, my hope is that you can take a good company to a great one, or better, a great one to a dominant one. Or, if you have a service or product within a company, you can improve upon it by saving your customer time or effort or improving the customer's overall experience.

There are so many little things that ultimately can add up to big things. Don't forget the importance of efficient navigation on your web-site. That might seem like a little thing, but for your prospects and customers, that can be a big thing. Remember, we are all impatient and a somewhat lazy and each web page and key stroke counts.

The purpose for writing this book is to point out what to some may be obvious, but to others it offers a new perspective and one that might be counter-intuitive. For those that challenge the status quo and work from the customer backward, they shall indeed reap the rewards of being part of a company that can grow tremendously and dominate their market and their competition.

95004699R00133

Made in the USA
Lexington, KY
03 August 2018